Herbert Puchta and Jeff Stranks
with Richard Carter and Peter Lewis-Jones

English in Mind

✳ Student's Book 3

CAMBRIDGE
UNIVERSITY PRESS

	Unit	Grammar	Vocabulary	Pronunciation
Module 1 — People and animals	1 Best of British	Present simple/continuous review. Present perfect simple review.	Giving statistics & making generalisations. Making new friends.	Schwa /ə/ in prepositions & articles.
	2 Ways of talking	Past simple vs. present perfect simple.	Body language. *say* & *tell*. Everyday English. Phrasal verbs with *up*.	Sentence stress: rhythm in questions.
	3 A true friend	Past simple/continuous review. Time conjunctions. Past simple vs. past perfect simple.	Friends & enemies.	Linking sounds.
	4 A working life	Present perfect simple/ continuous review. *had better / should / ought to*	Jobs & work.	/ɔː/ (sh<u>or</u>t).
	Module 1 Check your progress			
Module 2 — Survival	5 Travel	Future review.	Travel. Movement.	/gənə/ (*going to*).
	6 Live forever!	Future predictions. First conditional review, *if* & *unless*. Time conjunctions.	Verbs with prepositions. Everyday English. Phrasal verbs with *into*.	Weak & strong forms of prepositions.
	7 Campaigning for survival	Present/Past passive review. Present perfect & future passive. Causative *have*.	*make* & *do*.	Stress pattern in *have something done*.
	8 Reality TV	*make, let, be allowed to*. Modal verbs of obligation, prohibition & permission.	Television. Extreme adjectives & modifiers. Collocations with *on*.	/aʊ / (all<u>ow</u>ed).
	Module 2 Check your progress			
Module 3 — Right and wrong	9 Good and evil	Verbs + gerunds/infinitives. Verbs with gerund & infinitive.	Noun suffixes. Belonging to a group.	Stress in nouns, adjectives & verbs.
	10 Getting into trouble	Second conditional review. First conditional vs. second conditional. *wish / if only* + past simple.	Crime. Everyday English. Phrasal verbs with *down*.	*I wish … & if only …*
	11 Two sides to every story	Linkers of contrast. Modal verbs for deduction in the present.	Problems.	/əʊ/ (th<u>ough</u>).
	12 Mysterious places	Indirect questions. Modal verbs for deduction in the past.	Phrasal verbs. Expressions with *be* + preposition.	*have* in *must have / might have / can't have / couldn't have*.
	Module 3 Check your progress			
Module 4 — Emotions	13 Love	Reported statements review. Reported questions review. Reporting verbs.	Appearance. Personality. Relationships.	Intonation in reported questions.
	14 Anger	Third conditional review. *wish / if only* + past perfect simple. *should / shouldn't have done*.	Anger. Everyday English.	*should / shouldn't have*.
	15 Fear	Defining & non-defining relative clauses. Articles.	Adjectives with prefixes. Phrasal verbs with *sit*.	Pausing in non-defining relative clauses.
	16 Happiness	*be used to* + gerund vs. *used to* + infinitive. Grammar of phrasal verbs.	*feel*. Expressions with prepositions.	Stress in phrasal verbs.
	Module 4 Check your progress			

Projects ● Pronunciation ● Speaking: additional material ● Irregular verbs and phonetic chart ● Wordlist

Speaking & functions	Listening	Reading	Writing
How you spend your money. Presenting statistics. Describing recently completed or unfinished actions. Cultural influences.	Statistics about teenagers in Britain. Interviews with foreign visitors in Britain.	Quiz about British teenagers. Interview with a foreign student. Culture: Cultural Influences.	Report about the lifestyle of your family and friends.
Problems of being deaf. Talking about recently completed actions. Body language. Exchanging information.	Information on communicating with deaf people. Interview about body language.	Sharing Silence. Story: Meeting up again.	Describing a friendship.
Telling a story. Talking about friendship. Discussion: a love story.	Ghost story.	Ghost story. Questionnaire: Are You a Loyal Friend? Fiction: *Staying Together*.	Rewriting a short story about a relationship.
Your future job. Describing recently completed / unfinished actions. A job interview.	Dialogue about a dream job. A job interview. Song: *So You Want to Be a Rock 'n' Roll Star*.	Future Jobs.	Job application letter.
Sailing alone. Space tourism. Talking about travel. Solo journeys.	Interview with Ellen MacArthur.	Britain's Solo Sailor. Space Tourists. Culture: Going it Alone.	Email about a trip.
Micro-chips in your brain. Discussing causes of stress.	Interviews about the secrets of long life.	Intelligent Machines. Story: Ben calls Caroline.	A composition about life in the future.
Organisations which help tribal people. Talking about life in the future. Crime stories.	Speeches about town development.	Tribes in Danger. Fiction: *But Was it Murder?*	Letter to a newspaper about plans to build a new hotel.
Reality TV. Talking about rules in your home.	Interview about reality TV. Song: *Somebody's Watching Me*.	Reality TV.	Magazine article about a new TV show.
Computer games. Exchanging information. Graffiti.	Dialogue about a computer game.	Introductions of classic novels. Culture: The Writing's on the Wall.	Discursive composition: advantages & disadvantages.
Discussing getting into trouble. Describing hypothetical situations. Discussing crime. Things you wish could be different.	Dialogue about doing something wrong. Interviews about teenage crime.	Questionnaire: Are You Really Honest? Story: A problem for Matt.	Formal letter of opinion.
Discussing the making of the film *The Beach*. Discussing conspiracy theories. Hypnotism.	Radio programme about the first moon landing.	The making of the film *The Beach*. Fiction: *The Real Aunt Molly*.	Discursive composition: giving your opinion.
Mysterious places. Indirect questions. Speculating about Seahenge.	Interview about Seahenge. Song: *The Curse of the Mummy's Tomb*.	No One Knows Why They're There.	Narrative: setting a scene.
Giving & receiving presents. Describing someone. Weddings in your country.	Description of the film *The English Patient*.	*The Gift of the Magi*. Culture: Wedding Ceremonies.	Description of a person.
Something you regret doing. Talking about things that make you angry.	Dialogues about getting angry.	Regrets.com. Story: Working things out.	Narrative.
Discussing scary films. A ghost story.	Description of the film *The Blair Witch Project*.	The Fear in All of Us. Fiction: *The Lady in White*.	Film review.
The 'flow' of happiness. Talking about your idea of happiness.	Dialogues about being happy. Song: *Thank You*.	The 'Flow' of Happiness.	Poem.

Module 1
People and animals

YOU WILL LEARN ABOUT ...

- Teenage life in Britain ....
- Today's multicultural Britain ....
- Sign language and body language ....
- Animal friendship ....
- Choosing a career ....
- Manufactured rock bands ....

 Can you match each picture with a topic?

YOU WILL LEARN HOW TO ...

Speak

- Talk about how you spend your time and money
- Present statistics
- Describe recently completed or unfinished actions
- Discuss influences from different cultures
- Discuss problems of being deaf
- Describe recently completed actions
- Discuss how body language helps communication
- Talk about friendship
- Discuss your future job
- Have a job interview
- Discuss manufactured pop bands

Write

- A report about the lifestyles of your family and friends
- A description of a friendship
- Rewrite a short story about a relationship
- A job application letter

Read

- A quiz about British teenagers
- An interview with a foreign student
- An article about cultural influences in Britain
- An article about two deaf teenagers
- A ghost story
- A questionnaire about friendship
- An extract from a love story
- Short texts about future careers

Listen

- Some facts about life in Britain
- Interviews with visitors about their opinions of Britain
- Information about communicating with deaf people
- A radio interview about body language
- Part of a ghost story
- A conversation about a dream job
- A job interview
- A song

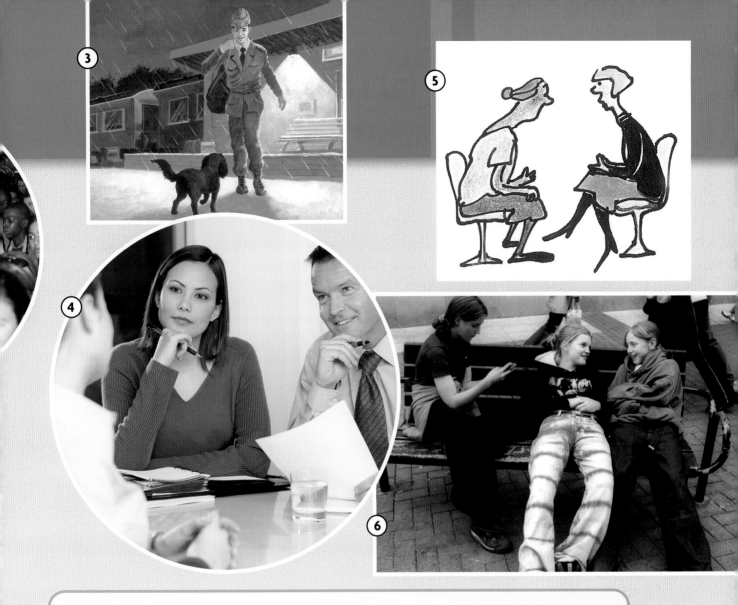

Use grammar

Can you match the names of the grammar points with the examples?

Present simple vs. present continuous

Past simple vs. present perfect simple

Present perfect simple vs. present perfect continuous

Time expressions

Past simple vs. past perfect simple

Past simple vs. past continuous

When he **turned** round, the dog **had disappeared**.

It **was raining** when the train **arrived**.

People **are using** the Internet more and more but I **prefer** books.

My friend **has decided** to study IT but **I've been thinking** about engineering.

My life **has changed** since I **met** him.

I had dinner **as soon as** I got home.

Use vocabulary

Can you think of two more examples for each topic?

Phrasal verbs with *up*	Expressions with *say* and *tell*	Jobs and work
look up	say a prayer	apply
turn up	tell a lie	employee
....	....	....
....	....	....

1 Best of British

* Present simple/continuous review
* Present perfect simple review
* Vocabulary: giving statistics and making generalisations
* Vocabulary: making new friends

1 Read and listen

(a) What images do you associate with Britain? Think of four adjectives to describe Britain and British people and explain your choices.

(b) Work with a partner and look at the quiz. Guess about British teenagers.

TEENAGERS IN BRITAIN

1 What percentage of the British population is under 16?
a 10%
b 20%
c 35%

2 What do most school-age teenagers say they enjoy?
a going to the cinema
b playing sport
c watching TV

3 How many 15–16-year-olds have the Internet at home?
a 1 in 2
b 1 in 7
c 1 in 13

4 How much is the average 11–16-year-old currently spending a week?
a £2
b £20
c £12

5 These days, teenagers are spending most of their money on:
a CDs
b mobile phone cards
c sweets

6 How many of Britain's 10–16-year-olds work part-time?
a 50,000
b half a million
c 2 million

7 What is the most common part-time work?
a babysitting
b paper round
c shop work

8 How many young people under 19 are living with just one parent?
a 5%
b 15%
c 25%

9 How many young people run away from home each year?
a 1,000
b 10,000
c 100,000

(c) 🔊 Listen and check your answers.

(d) 🔊 Listen again and mark the statements T (true) or F (false). Correct the false statements.

1 Watching TV is what teens usually do on a day they don't enjoy. ☐

2 The number of teens with Internet access at home is low, but increasing every day. ☐

3 Boys spend more money than girls. ☐

4 Schoolchildren with part-time jobs earn an average of £14 a month. ☐

Discussion box

Work in pairs or small groups. Discuss these questions together.

1 What do you enjoy doing in your free time?

2 Do you do anything to get spending money? What?

3 What do you spend your money on?

2 Grammar

Present simple vs. present continuous review

(a) Look at the examples. Then complete the rule.

*People **are using** the Internet more and more.*

*Two million teenagers **work** part-time.*

Rule:

- We use .... for permanent situations or facts.
- We use .... for regular habits or routines (that stay the same for a long time).
- We use .... for actions happening now, or around now.
- We use .... for changing situations and trends.

(b) Underline the examples of the present simple and present continuous in the quiz in Exercise 1. Why do you think each one is used?

(c) Finish these sentences about changes and trends in your country. Choose from the topics in the box.

| music | fashion | sport |
| hobbies | computers | TV |

1 More and more people my age *are spending their money on magazines.*

2 Teenagers ....
....

3 People in my country ....
....
....

4 My parents ....
....

3 Vocabulary

Giving statistics and making generalisations

Most More and more 1 in 3			have (a mobile phone). do (sport once a week). like (watching TV). think (shopping) is better than (seeing friends). prefer (sweets) to (CDs). tend to (spend their free time with friends).
A lot The majority (Just over/under) 10% (Over/under) a quarter (More/less than) half (About/around/almost) two thirds	of	girls/boys young people teenagers	
It is quite (un)common	for		to (have a TV in their bedroom).

(a) 🔊 Listen to these sentences from the quiz answers, and complete them with words from the box.

1 Surprisingly, ... 15–16-year-olds have the Internet at home.

2 Girls .... £2 a week more than boys.

3 It is .... 10–16-year-olds to have some kind of job.

(b) Work with a partner. Choose two of the following categories and write three questions for each one.

| sport | music | food | shopping | entertainment |

- Do you prefer ... to ...?
- Do you like ...?
- How often do you ...?
- What kind of ...?
- Do you ever ...?
- What do you usually ...?

(c) Take turns to ask your questions to all your classmates, but don't repeat anyone else's question! Note your answers, and then present them to the class, using language from the table above.

4 Pronunciation

Schwa /ə/ in prepositions and articles

🔊 Turn to page 120.

5 Read

Pietro is a student from Italy. He is studying in England. Read the interview and match the questions with Pietro's answers. Write A–H in the spaces. There is one question you do not need to use.

A Do you miss your family and friends?

B Is there anything about this country that surprises you?

C Do you like the food here?

D What do you think of the weather?

E Is it going to be hard for you to study different subjects in another language?

F How long have you been in Britain, Pietro?

G How long do you think you'll stay?

H Some people say that the British can be very cold. What do you think about that?

What do you think about England?

1 F
Since the beginning of summer. I've just finished an English course to prepare me for A-Levels.

2 _____
Well, yes, I suppose it is! But I'm going to take Maths and Computing A-Levels, so maybe my English doesn't need to be so perfect!

3 _____
No, not at all! I'm joking – of course I do. It's very difficult when I think about what my friends are doing right now – they're probably on the beach, having fun without me. Actually, my mother has been here for two weeks. She's visiting – I think she's making sure I'm eating properly!

4 _____
You mean the fish and chips? You know, I still haven't had any! Well, I have to say that it's not so good here at the school – the sandwiches taste a bit like plastic. I hope they can't hear me in the kitchen! But I'm staying with a really cool family, and I think they eat pretty good food, really – a lot of salads, a lot of pasta. It's not so different from home. Even my mum likes it!

5 _____
Well, yes, there's one thing. I knew before I came here that the British like football, but I didn't realise how much! Everyone has a favourite team, and all the girls seem to be in love with Wayne Rooney. I haven't seen a game yet, but I'll go soon. And I can't believe the horrible coffee, and the ice cream – sometimes it's OK, but everywhere you go in Italy it's fantastic.

6 _____
People back home said it was hard to make friends here, but I've only been here for three months and I've already made some really good 'mates', as they say here. At first, people don't want to talk to you much, but then they get to know you, and it's fine.

7 _____
Oh, I don't know. I haven't thought about it yet. If I like it maybe I could stay longer, but I can think about that later. I think I need to take the IELTS test first, so I have to make my English a little better. Who knows, I might never leave!

6 Listen

🔊 Listen to these short interviews with foreigners in Britain and complete the table.

	Reason for being in UK	Likes	Doesn't like
Gözde (Turkish)	_____	_____	weather
Marco (German)	_____	fashion	_____
Chris (American)	holiday	_____	_____
Rebecca (Venezuelan)	_____	_____	_____

Gözde

Marco

Chris

Rebecca

7 Grammar

Present perfect simple with *for* and *since* review

a Look at the examples. Why is the present perfect simple used? When do we use *for* and when do we use *since*?

*My mother **has been** here **since** the beginning of summer.*
*I **have been** in Britain **for** two weeks.*

b For each sentence below, two answers are correct and one is incorrect. Cross out the incorrect answer.

1	My life has changed since ...	~~more than a month~~	I met him	I went to Spain.
2	I haven't seen him for ...	a couple of weeks	such a long time	I was born.
3	I've had this photo for ...	the last six weeks	most of my life	the first time I saw you.
4	We haven't spoken since ...	Frankie's party	as long as I can remember	last Friday.

Present perfect with *just, already, yet* and *still*

c Complete the sentences from the text in Exercise 5.

1 I've .... finished an English course.
2 I .... haven't had any!
3 I haven't seen a game ....
4 I've .... made some really good mates.

d Complete the rule.

> **Rule:**
> - We use .... at the end of questions and negative sentences, to show that the speaker is expecting something to happen.
> - We use .... in positive sentences, to say something happened a short time ago.
> - We use .... in the middle of a sentence to say something happened sooner than expected.
> - We use .... in negative sentences before *haven't/hasn't* to show a feeling of surprise.

e Complete the sentences with *just, already, yet* or *still*.

1 I'm not hungry because I've .... had lunch.
2 I wrote to her last week. She hasn't replied ....
3 I wrote to her last week. She .... hasn't replied.
4 A: Don't forget to do your homework.
   B: I've .... done it!
5 Has it stopped raining ....?

8 Speak

a Work with a partner. Ask and answer *How long ...?* questions using the prompts below. Answer with *for* or *since*.

A: *What football team do you support, and how long have you supported them?*

B: *I've supported Bayern Munich since I was a baby / for a year or two.*

best friend	clothes	hobbies	possessions

b Read the list below. Guess if your partner has done these things and respond. Use *just, already, yet* or *still*.

A: *I think you've already cooked a meal for your family.*

B: *No, not yet. I hate cooking!*

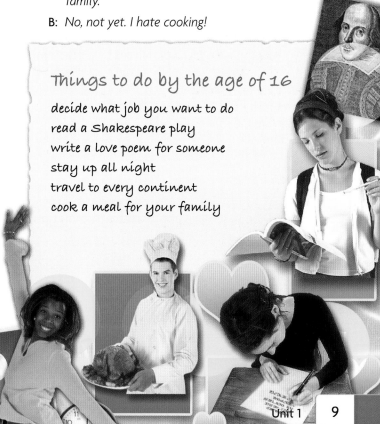

Things to do by the age of 16

decide what job you want to do
read a Shakespeare play
write a love poem for someone
stay up all night
travel to every continent
cook a meal for your family

Culture in mind

9 Read

(a) Read the text quickly. How many countries are mentioned?

Cultural Influences

Britain has a long history of influence from foreign cultures. The Romans started the trend 2000 years ago, when they invaded the country. More recently, immigrants have come from war-torn countries such as Iraq, Afghanistan and Bosnia. Some people in Britain are worried that immigration levels are too high, but for each of the last forty years more people have left the country than have immigrated there. Most immigrants these days come from Europe, North America and Australasia, not the poorer countries of Africa and Asia. The black and Asian population of Britain is only 6% of the total population, and over half of these were born in Britain – they are not immigrants.

Many immigrants in the UK live in London, where over 300 different languages are spoken in schools. You might be surprised to learn that there are more people living in London who were born in Germany, Italy, France or Spain than people who were born in Bangladesh or Pakistan.

Bend It Like Beckham is the story of an Asian girl living in suburban Britain who wants to play football, not cook traditional Indian food. She joins in with the boys, until she bonds with a girl who plays football for a girls' team. But for young British people, this film is not only about fitting in to a different culture, but also about what it's like to be young, to have parents who don't understand your dreams. *East Is East* is another British film comedy about a British Pakistani family in the North of England. People loved it for its accurate representation of life in Britain in the 1970s.

Benjamin Zephaniah is one of Britain's most popular contemporary poets. His parents were from Jamaica but he was born in Birmingham, England in 1958. At his first school, he felt left out because he was the only black boy. He settled in better at his next school, where he started performing his rhyme, rap and poetry in public. Nowadays, he is not afraid to talk about serious issues such as race and animal rights – he calls his poetry 'street politics' – but his poems are often very funny. They are very rhythmical, influenced by Jamaican music and dialect:

'Be nice to yu turkeys dis christmas,
Don't eat it, keep it alive,
It could be yu mate, an not on your plate
Say, Yo! Turkey I'm on your side.'

The immigrant population has had a big influence on the British music scene. West Indian culture and music inspired a number of British reggae bands such as UB40 in the 1980s, and in the 1990s Asian artists began to stand out. Cornershop's *Brimful of Asha* was a huge hit, and Talvin Singh became the first Asian to win the Mercury Music Prize. More recently artists such as Rishi Rich and Panjabi MC have successfully mixed traditional Asian Bhangra music with modern dance beats.

(b) Read the text again and find this information.

1 the original foreign influence on Britain
2 three places where people have emigrated from recently because of war
3 the number of languages spoken in London schools
4 the names of two films about Asian people living in Britain
5 the subject of the poem
6 the name of a British reggae band

Discussion box

Work in pairs or small groups. Discuss these questions together.

1 What other cultures influence music, literature, film and sport in your country?
2 Which country would you like to emigrate to?

10 Vocabulary

Making new friends

(a) Match the underlined expressions with definitions a–e.

1 Benjamin Zephaniah found it hard to <u>fit in</u> at his first school.
2 It's good to see the boys <u>bonding with</u> each other so well.
3 Come and <u>join in</u> the fun!
4 I sometimes <u>feel left out</u> because I'm no good at sports.
5 They <u>settled in</u> quickly to the area and made a lot of friends.

a feel like you belong to a group
b adapted to a new environment
c appear not to be included in a group
d participate in an activity
e linking emotionally to another person

(b) Put the letters in order to complete the questions, then discuss with a partner.

1 Would you ___settle in___ (tenstile) quickly if you went to live in another country, or would you miss home?
2 Do you .... (nifti) to all the different groups in your school?
3 Are there times when you .... (letfeetfoul) because you can't do something your friends can do?
4 If you find your friends playing a sport, do you just .... (ninijo) or do you wait to be asked?
5 Do you have any good friends that it took a long time to .... (windboth)?

11 Write

(a) Ayşe, a student from Izmir, has interviewed her family and friends about what is popular in Turkey. As you read her report, put these headings in the correct place:

Conclusion   Introduction   Findings

(b) Interview your friends and family and write a similar report. Use the vocabulary from Exercise 3a to help you. Write 120–150 words.

IMAGES OF TURKEY

1 ....

The aim of this report is to present what is popular in Turkey. I interviewed ten of my friends and all the people in my family, by telephone and in person. The questions concerned food, free time activities, sport and music.

2 ....

Food: Well over three-quarters prefer Turkish food – especially *meze* (lots of small dishes with vegetables in olive oil) – to food from other countries. About two-thirds like Turkish fast food, especially *pide* (Turkish pizza). Over half say their favourite drink is *ayran* (a yoghurt drink).

Free time: The majority of people like hanging out with friends and having picnics on the beach or in the park. All the adults like going to restaurants. More than half my friends go shopping every weekend. 40% play computer games every day.

Sport: Football is the most important sport for more than half of the people interviewed. About a quarter prefer basketball to football. A quarter of those interviewed said they didn't like sport.

Music: About three-quarters of my family prefer Turkish music to that from other countries. Among my friends, the majority usually listen to songs by British and American singers.

3 ....

The most surprising aspect of the report is that a large number don't like sport. I was also surprised to find out that it is quite common for my friends to listen to music in English.

2 Ways of talking

* Past simple vs. present perfect simple
* Vocabulary: *say* and *tell*
* Vocabulary: phrasal verbs with *up*

1 Read and listen

a Look at the words in the box. How do they communicate?

whales   people and their animals   deaf people

b Read the article quickly to find the answers to these questions.

1 How long have Orlando and German known each other?
2 What job do they do?

Sharing Silence

Deaf teenagers Orlando Chavez (16) and German Resendiz (17) have been friends since kindergarten. Together the two boys, who go to Escondido High School in California, have had the difficult job of learning in schools where the majority of the students can speak and hear.

Orlando lost his hearing at the age of one. German was born deaf, and his parents moved from Mexico to find a school where he could learn sign language. He met Orlando on their first day of kindergarten.

'We were in a special class with about 25 other deaf kids,' German remembers. 'Before then, I didn't know I was deaf and that I was different.'

'Being young and deaf in regular classes was very hard,' signs Orlando. 'The other kids didn't understand us and we didn't understand them. But we've all grown up together, and today, I'm popular because I'm deaf. Kids try hard to communicate with me.'

Some things are very difficult for the two boys. 'We can't talk on the phone, so if we need help, we can't call an emergency service,' German signs. 'And we can't order food in a drive-thru.'

Despite their difficulties, the two boys have found work putting food in bags at a local supermarket. They got their jobs through a 'workability' program, designed for teenagers from local schools with different types of learning disabilities.

German has worked in the supermarket since August, and Orlando started in November.

'The other people who work here have been very nice to us,' Orlando signs. 'They even sign sometimes. At first, we were nervous, but we've learned a lot and we're getting better.'

The opportunity to earn money has been exciting, both boys said. After high school, they hope to attend the National Technical Institute for the Deaf in New York.

c (🔊) Read the article again and listen. Mark the statements *T* (true) or *F* (false). Correct the false statements.

1 Orlando and German have both been deaf since they were born. ☐

2 As they have become older, it has become easier to communicate with their classmates. ☐

3 They say that one of their biggest problems is not being able to drive. ☐

4 The boys got their jobs at the supermarket through a special programme. ☐

5 Nobody at the supermarket is able to communicate with them. ☐

6 Both boys plan to work in the supermarket after they finish high school. ☐

Discussion box

Work in pairs or small groups. Discuss these questions together.

1 German mentions two problems he has. What other problems do you think deaf people have?

2 What jobs do you think would be easy for deaf people, and what would be impossible?

2 Listen

(🔊) Listen and take notes of four things to do if you want to communicate with a deaf person.

3 Grammar

Past simple vs. present perfect simple

a Look at the examples. Which of these sentences are in the past simple, and which are in the present perfect simple?

*They **have been** friends since kindergarten.*
*Orlando **lost** his hearing at the age of one.*
*German **met** Orlando on their first day of kindergarten.*
*German **has worked** in the supermarket since August.*

b Find other examples in the article in Exercise 1b. Underline examples in the past simple. Circle examples in the present perfect simple.

c Complete the rule. Write *past simple* or *present perfect simple*.

> **Rule:**
> - Use the .... to talk about events in the past which are separate from now (the moment of speaking).
> - Use the .... to connect the past and now (the moment of speaking).

*They **met** on the first day of kindergarten.*

*They **have been** friends since the first day.*

Time expressions

d Complete the rule. Write *past simple* or *present perfect simple*.

> **Rule:**
> - We use the .... with expressions such as *last week, a year ago, yesterday* (referring to time completely in the past).
> - We often use the .... with *for* and *since* (the period of time is from the past to now).
> - We usually use the .... with *just, already* and *yet* (words that have a link with now).
> - We often use the .... with *ever* and *never* (referring to any time up to now).

e Complete the text. Use the correct form of the past simple or the present perfect simple.

Sharon Adams ¹............... (leave) university in 1998 and ²............... (get) a job as an English teacher in Sweden. ³............... she .... (learn) the language? 'No, I ⁴............... (not learn) any Swedish while I was there!' she says. Since then, she ⁵............... (work) in four different countries, and she ⁶............... (write) two books for learners of English. Now she's a teacher in São Paulo. ⁷............... she .... (visit) Rio de Janeiro yet? 'Yes, I have. Last year I ⁸............... (spend) a month there, but so far I ⁹............... (not go) to any other places in Brazil yet. I plan to travel to the Amazon next July, though. I ¹⁰............... (save) $600 since my last holiday.'

4 Speak

a Work with a partner. Invent five things to impress them and write them down. Use the present perfect simple with *just*.

I've just met Eminem.

b Talk to your partner. Student A starts by telling Student B the first sentence. B quickly invents something that happened before, to impress A. Use the past simple.

Oh, really? He invited me to dinner last year, but I couldn't go.

A: *I've just bought a new car.*
B: *Oh, really? I bought a plane a week ago.*

5 Listening and vocabulary

Body language

a 🔊 Match the words with the pictures. Write 1–10 in the boxes. Then listen, check and repeat.

1	make eye contact	2	cross your arms
3	lean forward	4	sit back
5	avoid eye contact	6	gesture
7	raise your eyebrows	8	look nervous
9	give someone a warm smile	10	nod your head

b Work with a partner. Tick (✓) the things in Exercise 5a you think help communication and cross (X) the ones that do not help communication.

c 🔊 Listen to the interview with a psychologist, and choose answer a, b or c.

1 If someone crosses their arms, it could mean that they:
   a don't like you   b are bored with the conversation
   c are cold

2 90% of what we say:
   a is intelligent   b is done with our body language
   c is immediately forgotten

3 Mirroring is an example of how to:
   a communicate better   b make someone angry
   c look better

4 Mirroring works because:
   a we like people who look like us   b it's friendly
   c we like people who look good

5 The 'eyebrow flash':
   a takes about five seconds to do   b is a friendly greeting
   c shows that we don't like someone

6 The most important thing we can do to make people like us is:
   a smile at them   b make body contact with them
   c use the 'eyebrow flash' often

6 Speak

a Work with a partner.

Student A: Choose one of the topics in the box below. Talk to your partner about it for one minute.

Student B: Be a good listener.

Swap roles.

> something you bought recently
> an interesting film
> your plans for the next weekend
> your favourite place

b Now do the same thing with the other two topics, but this time be a bad listener.

c What difference did your body language make to communication?

7 Pronunciation

Sentence stress: rhythm in questions

🔊 Turn to page 120.

8 Vocabulary

say and *tell*

a Can you remember? All these sentences were said in the interview in Exercise 5c. Complete the sentences, using the correct form of *say* or *tell*.

1 If one person leans forward to _____ something, the other one leans forward too.

2 Can you _____ us another secret?

3 Well, when you meet someone you like, raise your eyebrows for up to one second – in this way your body is '_____' the other person that you like them.

4 Before we _____ 'good bye' – any other tricks you can _____ our listeners about?

5 Their bodies _____ , 'I hear you, I like you.'

b 🔊 Listen to the interview again and check your answers.

c Complete the sentences. Use the correct form of *say* and the words in the box.

> a prayer   (it) out loud   thank you
> sorry   (it) again   goodbye

1 Don't leave someone until you have _____ .

2 When people talk to God, they _____ .

3 When someone has done something for you, you should _____ .

4 When you have hurt somebody, you can make it better by _____ .

5 When you say what you're thinking so that people can hear, you _____ .

6 If someone didn't hear you, it helps to _____ .

d Complete these expressions by using the correct tense of *tell* with one of the words below.

> a lie   a joke   a secret   a story   the truth
> someone off   the time   the difference

1 My friend ___*told*___ me ___*a joke*___ yesterday – it was very funny, but now I can't remember it!

2 My watch has broken. Can you _____ me _____ , please?

3 One day when I was little, I _____ my parents _____ and they were very angry.

4 Can you _____ between an American accent and a British accent?

5 My teacher was so angry with me. She really _____ me _____ .

6 He says he's won medals for tennis, but I don't think he's _____ .

7 I'm going to _____ you _____ . Do you promise not to tell anyone else?

8 When I was little, my father used to _____ me _____ every night before I went to sleep.

9 Speak

Work with a partner. Student B: Turn to page 122.
Student A: Complete the questions with *say* or *tell*. Then ask your partner the questions. You start.

1 Did your parents always make you _____ 'please' and 'thank you' when you were younger?

2 How many times have you _____ 'I love you'?

3 Can you _____ me a funny joke?

4 Can you _____ what you did on your last three birthdays?

5 When was the last time you _____ a lie, and what was it?

Meeting up again

10 Read and listen

a 🔊 What news does Ben have for Matt? What is Joanne doing these days? Read, listen and check your answers.

Matt: Hey, Ben!

Ben: Matt! All right, mate? How's life?

Matt: Yeah, good. How's things with you? I haven't seen you for ages.

Ben: That's right. I think the last time we saw each other was – well, probably our last day at school.

Matt: That seems a long time ago. So, what about you? Where've you been all this time?

Ben: Well, I've been away. I've just got back from Hong Kong. My dad got a job there after we left school, so we all went out there to live. I've sort of lost touch with everyone.

Joanne: Matt, look, I've bought— Oh, Ben! Hi. Long time, no see. How are you?

Ben: Hi Joanne! I'm fine. I was just telling Matt about Hong Kong.

Joanne: Yeah, I heard you went there. What was that like?

Ben: Oh, it was pretty good at first, but things didn't work out between Mum and Dad, so I came back with my mum.

Matt: Oh, sorry to hear that, Ben.

Ben: Yeah, well. What can I do? Anyway, so what are you two doing with yourselves these days?

Joanne: We're both at college, but I'm kind of hoping to find a job in music somewhere.

Matt: Yeah, our band broke up, you know. I'm probably going to university next year, I don't know yet. What about you?

Ben: I'm not working at the moment. I don't know whether to try and go back to college or get a job. Nothing yet, though.

Joanne: Something will turn up.

Matt: Yeah, things'll work out. Anyway, listen, mate, we've got to be going. Let's meet up some time. Actually, I'm having a party tomorrow evening, if you're interested.

Joanne: Yeah, Caroline's coming – do you remember her?

Ben: Oh, yeah, of course. Well ... why not? It's great that I bumped into you two today. I wanted to look you up, but I don't have your numbers anymore.

Matt: Here, I'll give you it now.

Joanne: We've got to be going. Well, nice seeing you again, Ben.

Ben: Yeah, it is really good to see you, too.

Matt: See you tomorrow, mate. Take care.

b Answer the questions.

1 When did Ben and Matt last meet?
2 Where has Ben been?
3 What does Joanne want to do?
4 What is Ben unsure about?
5 What does Ben mean by 'bumped into'?

11 Everyday English

(a) Find expressions 1–8 in the story. Who says them?

1 all right, mate?   2 how's life/things?   3 long time, no see   4 anyway
5 (we've) got to be going   6 nice seeing you (again)   7 take care

Which ones are used:

a to open a conversation with someone you know well? ☐ ☐ ☐

b to bring a conversation to an end or say goodbye? ☐ ☐ ☐

c to change the direction or subject of a conversation? ☐

(b) Use one of the phrases to complete each sentence. There are two that you do not need.

1 A: ... And then suddenly this dog appeared!
   B: .... , about tomorrow night ...
2 A: Hi, James. .... ?
   B: Great. And .... with you?
3 A: Look at the time! Well, Steve, I've ....
   B: Me, too. Bye, Grace. It was ....

12 Vocabulary

Phrasal verbs with *up*

(a) Match the underlined verbs with the definitions a–d.

1 I wanted to look you up.   a appear, happen
2 Something will turn up.   b end a relationship
3 Let's meet up some time.   c visit or contact someone
4 Our band broke up.   d arrange to see someone

(b) Complete the sentences with one of the phrasal verbs from Exercise 12a, in the correct form.

1 I don't think we should ask them to the party – they've just .... with each other.
2 Well, goodbye – and if you ever come to London, please .... me ....
3 I left my camera on the train, but it .... at the Lost Property Office.
4 Listen, let's .... some time next weekend.

13 Write

(a) Read Kylie's composition about a person she has known for a long time. Do they see each other now? Read the text quickly to find out.

(b) Kylie uses two tenses in her composition. Which are they? Underline them in different colours.

My friend Rebecca

I have known my friend Rebecca for a long time. We first met at a friend's birthday party five years ago. We found out that we both liked techno and Green Day, so I invited Rebecca over to my place. We listened to my CDs together and soon became best friends.

Three years ago, Rebecca's parents invited me to go on holiday with them! It was great. We spent three wonderful weeks in a little cottage in Ireland. Rebecca and I loved walking along the beautiful beach. We took a lot of photos and had a lot of fun.

Two years ago I spent a week in hospital and Rebecca came to see me every day. But then, last year, Rebecca's father changed his job, and they moved to another town. Since then we haven't seen each other very much, but we've talked on the phone and we've written emails to each other.

(c) Think of a person you have known for a long time. Write about when you first met them and about some things you did together. Use Kylie's composition to help you. Write 120–150 words.

For your portfolio

③ A true friend

* Past simple vs. past continuous review
* Past simple vs. past perfect simple
* Time conjunctions
* Vocabulary: friends and enemies

1 Speak and read

(a) Do you know any stories, films, TV programmes or cartoons that involve dogs or other animals?

(b) Match the phrases with the pictures. Write 1–5 in the boxes.

1. a man fighting in a war
2. someone coming out of a train station
3. someone patting a dog on the head
4. a dog barking
5. someone dreaming of apple pie

(c) Work with a partner. Look at the pictures again and put them in order to tell the first part of the story.

(d) 🔊 Read, listen and check your ideas in Exercise 1c.

Old Shep

After two years fighting in the war, Hugh Davis was finally going home. As the train was travelling through the hills and valleys of Kentucky, Hugh thought of his mother's home-made apple pie and his faithful old dog Shep lying beside the fire.

It was already dark when the train arrived at the local station. It was raining hard and a strong wind was blowing. When Hugh came out of the railway station, Shep was there waiting for him. The man and the dog were happy to see each other. Hugh patted his dog on the head and together they started the three-mile walk home.

While they were walking, the storm got worse, and Hugh decided to take a short cut home, across the bridge over the river. As soon as he started to cross the bridge, Shep started barking loudly. Hugh stopped and looked round at Shep, but the dog kept barking furiously. Then Hugh looked down at the bridge.

(e) What do you think happened next? How do you think the story ends?

2 Grammar

Past simple vs. past continuous review

a Look at these two sentences from the story of Old Shep. Which verbs are in the past simple? Which verbs are in the past continuous?

*When Hugh **came** out of the railway station, Shep **was waiting** for him.*

*While they **were walking**, the storm **got** worse.*

b Find other examples like this from the text, and <u>underline</u> them. Then complete the rule. Write *past simple*, *past continuous*, *when*, and *while*.

> **Rule:**
> * We use the .... for an action that happened at one moment in the past. We often use .... with this tense.
> * We use the .... for a background action or description in the past. We often use .... with this tense.

c Complete the sentences with the correct form of the verbs.

1 My brother *was climbing* a tree when he ......*fell*...... and broke his leg. (climb, fall)
2 When my parents .... home, we .... a DVD. (come, watch)
3 Jordan .... while my sister .... some homework. (phone, do)
4 While I .... tennis, a ball .... me in the eye. (play, hit)
5 Kimberley .... the web when she .... a great new site. (surf, find)
6 While we .... on the beach, it .... to rain. (walk, start)

Time conjunctions: *as / then / as soon as*

d There are some other words that we often use with past simple or past continuous.

* as (= while)

   As the train was travelling through the hills and valleys of Kentucky ...

* as soon as (= at exactly the same moment)

   As soon as Hugh started to cross the bridge, Shep started barking.

* then (= the next moment)

   Then Hugh looked down at the bridge.

e Connect the sentences to make a story, using the word in brackets. Change the order of the sentence halves if necessary.

1 I left the cinema. I started walking home. (then)
   I left the cinema, then I started walking home.
2 I was walking. I heard a strange noise. (while)
3 I looked up. Something hit me on the head. (as)
4 The thing hit me. Everything went black. (as soon as)
5 I was lying in a hospital bed. I woke up. (when)
6 I rang the bell. A nurse came to talk to me. (as soon as)
7 The nurse was talking to me. I fell in love with her. (while)

f Complete the dialogue with the correct form of the verbs.

Lee: Hey Frances. I hear you played your first concert last night. How was it?

Frances: It was OK. The audience [1] ...*liked*... (like) it, I think. But we [2] .... (have) some problems!

Lee: Really? What [3] .... (happen)?

Frances: Well, as I [4] .... (sing) the fourth song, all the lights suddenly [5] .... (go) out!

Lee: Oh no! What [6] .... (you do)?

Frances: The audience sat in the dark and I carried on singing!

Lee: Wow! Well done – that was pretty cool of you.

Frances: Oh, that was nothing. As soon as the lights [7] .... (come) back on, I realised my microphone [8] .... (not work)! So while the guys [9] .... (fix) the microphone, the band played on, and when it was fixed I [10] .... (start) singing again. No problem!

Lee: No problem? Well, I hope all your concerts aren't like that.

Frances: Yeah, me too!

3 Speak and read

a) Work with a partner. Retell the story of *Old Shep*.

b) Read the second part of the story. What happened in the end?

When Hugh looked down, he saw that the middle part of the bridge had fallen into the river, and he could see the cold, fast-flowing water 30 metres below. When he turned round to thank Shep for saving his life, the dog had disappeared into the darkness.

When Hugh finally got home, his mother was waiting at the door to welcome him. They hugged each other and then sat down for supper. His mother had cooked him a wonderful dinner and had also made his favourite dessert – apple pie. While he was eating, Hugh told her how Shep had saved his life. Then he looked up at his mother: her face had gone white.

'When you left to fight in the war,' she said, 'it broke the dog's heart. Shep died two years ago, son.'

4 Listen

🔊 Listen to a girl telling the story of *Old Shep*. Write the five things that are different from the story you read.

5 Grammar
Past simple vs. past perfect simple

a) Look at these two sentences from the story. Answer the questions.

*He **saw** that the middle part of the bridge **had fallen** into the river.*

*When he **turned** round to thank Shep for saving his life, the dog **had disappeared** into the darkness.*

1 Did the bridge fall into the river when Hugh looked down, or before?

2 Did Shep disappear when Hugh turned round, or before he turned round?

b) Find other examples of the past perfect simple in the story in Exercise 3b, and underline them. Then complete the rule.

> **Rule:**
> ● We use the _____ to talk about an event that took place at a particular time in the past.
> ● We use the _____ when we need to make it clear that an event took place before another past event.

c) Complete the sentences with the correct form of the verbs.

1 When Mike _____ at the station, the train _____ . (arrive, leave)

2 The programme _____ when Tessa _____ on the TV. (finish, turn)

3 When they _____ home, the dog _____ their dinner. (get, eat)

4 Everybody _____ home when they _____ to the party. (go, get)

d) Complete the text with the correct form of the verbs.

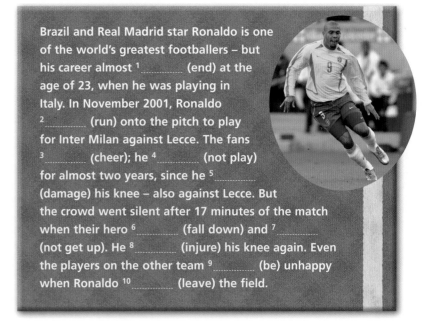

Brazil and Real Madrid star Ronaldo is one of the world's greatest footballers – but his career almost ¹_____ (end) at the age of 23, when he was playing in Italy. In November 2001, Ronaldo ²_____ (run) onto the pitch to play for Inter Milan against Lecce. The fans ³_____ (cheer); he ⁴_____ (not play) for almost two years, since he ⁵_____ (damage) his knee – also against Lecce. But the crowd went silent after 17 minutes of the match when their hero ⁶_____ (fall down) and ⁷_____ (not get up). He ⁸_____ (injure) his knee again. Even the players on the other team ⁹_____ (be) unhappy when Ronaldo ¹⁰_____ (leave) the field.

Are you a loyal friend?
TRY THIS AND SEE

6 Read

(a) Read the questionnaire and answer the questions.

1 Your friend has asked you to go to a party, but you want to watch something really good on TV. Do you:

a say you'll go to the party, but let your friend down by staying in and watching TV instead?

b go to the party anyway?

c tell your friend the truth and stay at home – you get on well with them, so it's no problem?

2 You hear people saying that a friend of yours has done something bad. Do you:

a not speak to your friend the next time you see them?

b carry on as normal and wait for your friend to explain?

c stick up for your friend by saying that they would never do anything like that?

3 Your friend asks to borrow your homework for the second time in a week. Do you:

a tell your teacher – you can't let friends copy like that?

b let them copy, of course?

c refuse, but offer to help your friend to do their own work?

4 Your friend has done something wrong, but people think it was you that did it. Do you:

a tell on your friend, so that they get into trouble, not you?

b just say you did it and stand by your friend; they would do the same for you?

c do your best to explain it wasn't you, and hope no one finds out that it was your friend?

5 Your friend is late meeting you at the cinema, and the film has already begun. Do you:

a go home angrily and fall out with your friend – that's the last time you'll invite them out!

b know that your friend always has a good reason, and forget about it?

c see the film anyway and, afterwards, try to find out what happened?

(b) Count how many a, b and c answers you have and check your score. Do you agree with it?

7 Vocabulary
Friends and enemies

Choose the best meaning for the <u>underlined</u> expressions from the questionnaire.

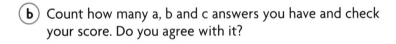

1	<u>let</u> your friends <u>down</u>	a) hit	b) disappoint
2	<u>get on well with</u> someone	a) argue a lot	b) have a good relationship
3	<u>stick up for</u> your friend	a) support	b) laugh at
4	<u>tell on</u> your friend	a) talk to	b) tell someone that your friend did something wrong
5	<u>stand by</u> your friend	a) don't speak to	b) be loyal
6	<u>fall out with</u> your friend	a) stop being friends	b) have a physical fight

Are you a loyal friend?

Mostly a answers:
You get on well with your friends but when things get tough, you disappear. Do you always let your friends down like this?

Mostly b answers:
When it comes to loyalty, you stand by your friends in any situation. Aren't you sometimes a little bit too trusting?

Mostly c answers:
You know how to balance loyalty with honesty – real friends want to know the truth, even when it hurts, don't they?

8 Pronunciation
Linking sounds

🔊 Turn to page 120.

9 Speak

Think of another question to test how loyal you are. Work with a partner. Compare and explain your answers to the questionnaire in Exercise 6a, and ask your own question. Use the vocabulary from Exercise 7.

Unit 3   21

Fiction in mind

10 Read

(a) Look at the title and the cover of the book. What kind of story is *Staying Together*?

Staying Together

by Judith Wilson

The story

Ikuko goes to England to study, promising Hiroshi she will return to Japan to get married. This is a powerful story of love that is carried across the continents ...

She remembered the day they'd met. It had been late on a Friday afternoon. She'd only been working there for a few weeks and she was still feeling unsure of herself. She was entering numbers on the computer for a sales program. But the results looked wrong. She took a deep breath and went up to Mr Honma's desk to tell him. Mr Honma hadn't been very helpful, but he'd arranged for one of the programmers to have a look.

Half an hour later Ikuko had looked up to see a tall man, young and with rather untidy hair, coming across the room towards her. He stopped and introduced himself.

'I'm Hiroshi Masuda. I hear you have some problems with the sales program,' he said.

Ikuko explained and Hiroshi listened carefully, then sat down and did some work on the computer. Suddenly he stopped and looked up at her, brushing his hair out of his eyes. He was excited. 'You're absolutely right. There's a mistake in the program. I knew there was something wrong with the numbers we were getting. Now we can change it. Thanks!' He stood up. 'Anyway, it's probably time you got off home. Do you live far away?'

'In Ome. It's an hour away on the train,' said Ikuko.

'Oh, yes, I know. In fact I go through Ome on my way home. So we've been travelling on the same train. I'm surprised we haven't seen one another before.'

'Well, the trains are so crowded,' Ikuko said.

'Yes,' he said, 'but I'd notice you, even in a crowd.'

And that was how it had begun. Sitting in the train now, two years later, Ikuko remembered the early days of their friendship: meals in small restaurants, walks in the park – slowly getting to know each other. They discovered that they'd both gone to the same Junior High school, although Hiroshi had been four years ahead of Ikuko. After leaving university, he'd gone to do a computing course in America. He'd done very well, but hadn't enjoyed life in America and decided instead to return to Tokyo.

In those first days of new love, Ikuko and Hiroshi had spent almost all their free time together. Ikuko liked his gentleness and understanding. It was the perfect relationship. No arguments or bad surprises. Wasn't that what she wanted?

'Ome … Ome.' Ikuko heard the name of her station and woke suddenly from her thoughts. She got off and walked out of the crowded station. On her way home, she stopped at a department store – she still had to buy a suitcase for her trip.

★ ★ ★

A few days later Ikuko was sitting in Narita International Airport with Hiroshi. The blue suitcase had already been checked in on the London flight, and they were having one last coffee together.

The two of them had hardly spoken on the way to the airport. Ikuko wondered if she was making a terrible mistake. 'It's only for six months,' she said to Hiroshi, trying to persuade herself as much as him.

'A lot can happen in six months,' he said. 'I don't want to lose you. Remember you promised to come back.'

11 Write

(a) Read the story. Where did Adam and Jessica meet? What happened to Jessica?

Jessica and Adam met five years ago. She was working in London[1]. One day she saw him[2]. He was a university student, but was doing a summer job[3]. He had come to the place where she was working[4].

As Adam was leaving, he left a little message next to Jessica's computer[5]. Jessica phoned him[6] and they met the same evening. Adam and Jessica liked each other a lot[7]. One day a terrible thing happened. Jessica was hit by a car[8]. She was badly hurt. Six months later Jessica was OK again. Adam had helped her a lot[9].

(b) Read the extract from the story. Choose answer a, b or c.

1 Ikuko and Hiroshi met for the first time:
   a at the airport   b at high school
   c at work

2 Ikuko first realised that Hiroshi was attracted to her:
   a after he tried to fix her computer
   b when he saw her on his train
   c after their first meal together

3 We discover that Ikuko and Hiroshi went to the same:
   a computing course   b high school
   c university

4 Ikuko liked Hiroshi because he:
   a was kind and considerate   b was funny
   c gave her lots of surprises

5 At the airport, they probably felt:
   a happy about Ikuko's trip
   b angry with each other
   c worried and unsure

Discussion box

Work in pairs or small groups. Discuss these questions together.

1 Do you like reading love stories? Why / Why not?

2 What do you think happens in the end?

(b) Rewrite the story in 120–150 words. Use these questions to make the story more interesting. Remember to use linking words like *when* and *while*.

1 What was she working as?
2 Where did she see him?
3 What was he working as?
4 Where exactly was she working?
5 What did the message say?
6 When did she phone him?
7 What did they like about each other?
8 What was she doing at that moment?
9 How had Adam helped her?

For your portfolio

4 A working life

✳ Present perfect simple vs. present perfect continuous review
✳ *had better / should / ought to*
✳ Vocabulary: jobs and work

1 Read and listen

(a) Look at the photographs and answer the questions.

1   What jobs do the people in photos **a** and **b** have?
2   What industries do the people in photos **c** and **d** work in?

(b) A magazine asked teenagers about their future job intentions. Here is what four of them said. Read the article quickly. Match the teenagers with the jobs.

Future Jobs

Rob (17) from Lincoln

My dream is to go into information technology. My school doesn't teach much IT but I've been doing a programming course at home in my own time. I think a job in IT will be very challenging, but that's what I like – new things to try, to learn. I hope to go to the States and live and work there, maybe Silicon Valley. That's where the well-paid jobs are – and a good salary's important, isn't it?

Lauren (16) from Norwich

I've always wanted to be an engineer. That's what my father does. I need a university degree of course, and that's fine. I've already started learning though – my father invites me to come with him sometimes, so I've been spending my holidays watching what he does. It's fascinating, I can't wait to be an engineer myself.

Mark (16) from Oxford

A lot of my friends have decided to study IT at university – they think they can get well-paid jobs that way. I'm not sure. It's not always easy to do well in that area, because there's a lot of competition. I've been thinking about working in banking. It's not very exciting I suppose, but I think it's a safe career. That's important for me. I've written letters to three or four banks to see what kind of opportunities they have.

Gemma (17) from Leeds

My future job? Well, I know I want to work with children. Maybe teaching, because I think it's probably a very rewarding job, you're helping people, you know? I know it's usually badly paid, but that's not the important thing for me. I've been visiting a primary school for the last few weeks, on work experience, and it's been really interesting. Yeah, probably teaching.

(c) 🔊 Read the texts again and listen. Answer the questions.

1   Who wants to do the same job as their father?
2   Who wants to work with children?
3   Who thinks earning a lot of money is important? Who doesn't think so?
4   Who doesn't need an exciting job?
5   Who wants to work in another country?
6   All four of them have already done things about their future jobs. What things?

Discussion box

Work in pairs or small groups. Discuss these questions together.

1   How important is money for you when you choose your future job?
2   What other things are important for your choice?
3   Are there any jobs that you definitely wouldn't want to do? Which? Why?
4   What have you been doing in order to get the job you want in the future?

2 Grammar

**Present perfect simple
vs. continuous review**

a Look at the examples. Then complete the rule.

A lot of my friends **have decided** *to study IT
at university.*
I've been thinking about working in banking.
*I've been visiting a primary school for the last
few weeks.*

> **Rule:** Write *simple* or *continuous*. Use the
> examples above to help you.
> - We use the present perfect .... to
>   show that an action is now completed. The
>   focus is on the result. We also use it to say
>   how often something happened.
> - We use the present perfect .... to
>   talk about an action that started in the past
>   and that may or may not be completed.
>   The focus is on the action and how long it
>   has been in progress.

b Now find other examples in the text and
<u>underline</u> them.

c Complete the sentences with the verbs in the box.

> written   been playing   read   been reading
> ~~played~~   been writing

1   I'm not surprised the players are tired – they've
    ...*played*... four matches this week.
2   My sister's .... five letters since breakfast
    – I wonder who they're to?
3   My fingers hurt! I've .... emails on my
    computer all morning.
4   I've .... this page three times already,
    but I still don't understand it.
5   Can we stop now? We've .... this game
    for more than an hour, and I'm bored!
6   I've .... this book for hours, and I'm still
    only on page 5.

d Match the questions 1–7 with replies a–g.
Complete the sentences with the correct form
of the verbs.

1   Do you want a chocolate?
2   Why's your sister so angry?
3   Do you want to watch *Titanic*?
4   Why is your father so tired?
5   Is it alright if I go out now, Mum?
6   Does your sister speak French?
7   How's the homework going?

3 Speak

Work with a partner. Take turns to start
a new conversation.

Tell your partner about:	Your partner asks you questions:
- your favourite piece of clothing	How long ...? (have it)
- something you are learning/studying	How long ...? (learn/study it)
- the place where you live	How long ...? (live there)
- a book you are reading	How long ...? (read it)
- a good friend of yours who is not in your class	How long ...? (know them)

Look

have (= possess) and *know* are not
normally used in the continuous form.

*I **have known** her for three years.*

(Not: ~~I have been knowing her for three
years.~~)

a   Not very well. I still .... (not finish).
b   No thanks, I .... (eat) four today already!
c   Wait a minute. .... (clean) your room?
d   Only a little. She .... (not learn) for very long.
e   She .... (argue) with her boyfriend all day.
f   I don't know. .... (work) in the garden?
g   OK. Can you believe I .... (not see) it before!

4 Listen

(a) Look at the picture of Claire and her bedroom. What can you say about her interests?

(b) Read the conversation. What is Claire excited about? What advice does Grace give?

Grace: Hey, Claire! Listen to this ¹＿＿＿＿ . 'Ambitious young designer with excellent computing skills needed. Salary £1,500 a month. Phone or email for an ²＿＿＿＿ .' Sounds brilliant! That's what you've always wanted to do.

Claire: Well, I'm not sure, really.

Grace: What? But it's always been your dream to become a designer! You should phone them and ask for an application form. And you should ³＿＿＿＿ and send your ⁴＿＿＿＿ . Oh, and tell them about all the courses you've done. Then they'll call you for an ⁵＿＿＿＿ and you'll get the ⁶＿＿＿＿ !

Claire: Grace? Can you keep a secret?

Grace: Of course.

Claire: You know my band? We've got a gig at The Ballroom and we're supporting *Muse*.

Grace: You're joking!

Claire: No, it's completely true. I promise. That's why I don't want a ⁷＿＿＿＿ as a designer any more.

Grace: But Claire – you ought to think about your future. You really should think twice.

Claire: Well, I am thinking about my future. That's why I'm doing what I'm doing.

Grace: You know – I think you'd better talk to Mum and Dad about all this!

(c) 🔊 Read the conversation again and complete the dialogue with the words in the box. Then listen and check.

> advertisement   interview   fill it in   career
> application form   job   CV

(d) Work with a partner and discuss these questions:

1 What do you think of Claire's plans?
2 What do you think Claire's parents will say?

(e) 🔊 Listen to Claire talking to her parents. Were you right?

5 Grammar

had better / should / ought to

(a) Can you remember what advice Grace gave her sister? Complete the sentences. Then check your answers.

1 You ＿＿＿＿ think about your future.
2 You really ＿＿＿＿ think twice.
3 I think you ＿＿＿＿ talk to Mum and Dad.

> **Rule:**
> - We use *should* or *ought to* to give general advice and opinions. They have a similar meaning.
> - We use *'d better* to give advice for a specific situation. There is the idea that there will be a problem if the advice is not followed. It is always used in the past form (not ~~have~~ better).

Look

*You'd better = You **had** better*
(Not: ~~You would better~~)
The negative is *had better not.*

(b) Complete the sentences with the correct form of *should, ought,* or *better.*

1 'I've got an exam tomorrow. I think I'd ＿*better*＿ get a good night's sleep.'
2 'Your hair looks terrible – you ＿＿＿＿ to go to the hairdresser's.'
3 'Listen, it's really late. I think we ＿＿＿＿ leave soon.'
4 'I'm not surprised she's angry – you ＿＿＿＿ talk to people in that way!'
5 'OK, you can borrow my camera – but you'd ＿＿＿＿ lose it!'
6 'If you want a good career, you ＿＿＿＿ to work harder at school!'

6 Pronunciation

/ɔː/ *short*

🔊 Turn to page 120.

7 Vocabulary

Jobs and work

(a) 🔊 Match the definitions 1–10 with the expressions a–j. Then listen, check and repeat.

1   to write a letter to ask for a job
2   a person who works in a company
3   someone who gives other people a job
4   done for the whole of the working week
5   done for part of the working week
6   official records showing you have finished a training course or you have skills
7   to say that you want to leave a job
8   the money you get paid every month for doing your job
9   a person who is learning how to do a job
10 not having a job / out of work

a   full-time (job)
b   unemployed
c   part-time (job)
d   trainee
e   resign
f   salary
g   employee
h   apply for a job
i   qualifications
j   employer

(b) Complete the questions using expressions from Exercise 7a.

1   A: 'Is your job __*full-time*__ ?'
    B: 'Yes, 40 hours like everybody else.'

2   A: 'Is he still _____ ?'
    B: 'Yes, he has been out of work for two years.'

3   A: 'Is your _____ good?'
    B: 'Not really. I only get £400 a month.'

4   A: 'Why did you _____ this job?'
    B: 'Because I thought it seemed really interesting.'

5   A: 'Why did he _____ ?'
    B: 'Because he found a better job with another company.'

6   A: 'Is your job _____ ?'
    B: 'Yes, I only work twelve hours a week.'

7   A: 'How many _____ have you got?'
    B: 'More than 400. And they're doing a good job.'

8   A: 'Do you have any _____ ?'
    B: 'Yes, I passed my teaching exams in 1997.'

9   A: 'What's the name of your last _____ ?'
    B: 'I worked for British Airways.'

10 'For the first six months you will work as a _____ while you learn to do the job.'

8 Listen

🔊 Listen to the job interview. Make notes under these headings:

● Job wanted   ● Experience
● Current job   ● Qualifications

9 Speak

Work with a partner. Choose a job together from these advertisements and have a job interview. One of you is the interviewer, the other is the applicant (the person who wants the job). Then swap roles and choose a different job. Think about:

● reasons for application (Why / apply?)
● qualifications (What kind of qualifications / have?)
● expected salary (What salary / expect?)
● currently employed (What kind of job / do?)

Teacher for inner-city school required

Subjects: English, Geography and P.E.

WANTED:

IT Expert for company developing software programs

WANTED

SALES ASSISTANT for delicatessen in supermarket

Engineer for car manufacturing company required

10 Speak and listen

a Work with a partner. In the box are some things that rock stars do. What other things do they do?

> write some songs   sign autographs
> find an agent   sign a contract

b 🔊 Listen to the song and complete the sentences.

The Byrds

Did you know ...?
This song was written in 1967 by Chris Hillman and Roger McGuinn. They were part of the popular American band *The Byrds*, who were sometimes called the American Beatles. They wrote the song about another popular band at that time, *The Monkees*, who were specially created for a TV series. They didn't play any instruments or write any songs.

The Monkees

So You Want To Be A Rock 'n' Roll Star

by The Byrds

So you want to be a rock 'n' roll star?
Then listen now to what I [1] _____
Just get an electric [2] _____
Then take some time
And learn how to [3] _____
And with your hair swung right
And your pants too tight
It's gonna be [4] _____

Then it's time to go downtown
Where the agent man won't let you down
Sell your soul to the [5] _____
Who are waiting there to sell plastic ware
And in a [6] _____ or two
If you make the charts
The girls'll tear you apart

What you paid for your riches and fame
Was it all a strange [7] _____ ?
You're a little insane
The [8] _____ , the game, and the public acclaim
Don't forget what you are
You're a rock 'n' roll star!

c Match the expressions 1–6 with definitions a–f.

1 the price you pay   a don't do something too quickly
2 take some time   b disappoint you
3 sell your soul   c let someone control you completely
4 let you down   d what happens when a lot of people buy your song
5 public acclaim   e the cost of having success
6 make the charts   f when a lot of people say they like what you do

Discussion box

Work in pairs or small groups. Discuss these questions together.

1 Do you think *The Byrds* admired *The Monkees*?

2 What band can you think of today that this song could be about?

11 Write

(a) Read Sophie's job application. What job is she applying for?

(b) Read the letter again and answer the questions.

1 Where does Sophie write her name, and where does she write her address?
2 Where does she put the date?
3 How does she start the main part of the letter? What do you write if you know the name of the person you are writing to, for example Richard Clark or Deborah Jenkins?
4 In which paragraph does she state what her reason for writing is?
5 How does she organise her reasons for believing that she is the right person for the job?
6 How does she end the letter? What do you write if you know the name of the person you are writing to?

123 South Street
Rochester
Kent ME8 7BY

Tel: 01889 389456
solake@freespace.co.uk

23 June, 2005

Personnel Department
e-Style
Romsey Street
Birmingham B60 3DH

Dear Sir or Madam

I read your advertisement for a web designer in yesterday's *Times* and would like to apply. I enclose my CV as requested. I think there are several reasons why I might be the right person for the job.

First of all, I have always been fascinated by technology. I got my first computer when I was eight, and I have been interested in the Internet since then. I created my own website at the age of 14, and since then I have been designing websites for my friends.

Secondly, I believe I have the right qualifications. I have taken several courses in IT, including specialist courses in Java and Flash. I was an assistant for a web design studio for six weeks during the summer holidays. I have been working part time for the same studio since then, as well as being a student.

Lastly, I would like to stress that I would love to work in a team with other people who have more experience than me. I would love to improve my skills through learning from others. I am very willing to work hard, and I do not mind working overtime.

I can be contacted by phone or email for an interview. I look forward to hearing from you.

Yours faithfully

Sophie Lake

Sophie Lake

(c) Write a letter of application in answer to one of the advertisements in Exercise 9. Remember to say which job you are applying for and where you saw the advertisement. Use Sophie's letter to help you. Write 120–150 words.

Module 1 **Check your progress**

1 **Grammar**

a Complete the sentences. Use the present simple or present continuous form of the verbs.

1 My parents ___tend___ (tend) to watch TV in the evenings.
2 I _____ (work) in a music shop at the moment.
3 I _____ (prefer) vegetarian food to meat.
4 _____ he _____ (go) swimming every morning?
5 The majority of teenagers _____ (not like) doing homework.

| | 4 |

b Complete the sentences. Use the correct form of the present perfect simple and *for, since, just, already, yet* or *still.*

1 Hi! I ___haven't seen___ (not see) you ___since___ last summer.
2 Be careful! I _____ (paint) that door.
3 He _____ (not be) to school _____ three days.
4 Wait! I _____ (not finish) eating my dessert _____ !
5 Not *Titanic* again! We _____ (see) it four times.
6 Where are you going? You _____ (not clean) your room.

| | 5 |

c Complete the sentences. Use the correct form of the past simple or present perfect simple.

1 I___'ve never had___ (never have) a surprise birthday party.
2 I _____ (leave) school last June.
3 Why _____ you _____ (not tell) me yesterday?
4 I still _____ (not send) an email to Dave. I'll do it now.
5 How long _____ she _____ (have) that piercing? It looks new.
6 _____ you _____ (go) to the cinema last night?

| | 5 |

d Complete the sentences. Use the correct form of the past simple and past continuous.

1 Somebody ___called___ (call) you while you ___were walking___ (walk) the dog.
2 While they _____ (build) this house, they _____ (find) some ancient coins.
3 I _____ (write) this song while I _____ (wait). What do you think?
4 Why _____ everyone _____ (talk) about me when I _____ (get) to school?
5 Somebody _____ (climb) out of the window, when the police _____ (arrive).
6 I _____ (not find) your glasses while I _____ (clean).

| | 5 |

e Complete the sentences. Use the correct form of the past simple and past perfect.

1 That ___was___ (be) the first time I ___had met___ (meet) her.
2 We _____ (not be) hungry because we _____ (eat) lunch already.
3 Everyone _____ (go) to bed when I _____ (get) home.
4 We _____ (arrive) late but luckily the film _____ (not start).
5 They _____ (take) my plate away but I _____ (not finish) eating!
6 _____ Jon _____ (see) the film before? Yes – he _____ (see) it last week.

| | 5 |

f Complete the sentences. Use the correct form of the present perfect simple or continuous.

1 Sorry! How long ___have___ you ___been waiting___ (wait) for me?
2 I _____ (write) ten emails this morning.
3 _____ you _____ (see) my keys anywhere?
4 I _____ (not learn) Japanese very long, but I know lots of words already.
5 Sorry, I _____ (not finish) my homework.
6 Have you looked outside? It _____ (snow) all night!

| | 5 |

8 Rewrite the sentences, using the words in brackets.

1 It would be a good idea if you took an umbrella.

You _had better take an umbrella_ . (had better)

2 Why don't you tell the truth?

You _____ . (ought)

3 Don't sit there!

You _____ . (shouldn't)

4 Don't you think it would be a good idea to stop now?

Hadn't _____ . (better)

5 She ought to apologise.

She _____ . (should)

☐ **4**

2 Vocabulary

a Complete the sentences with the words in the box.

> of   in   for   ~~out~~   about
> up   with

1 I sometimes feel left _out_ because I don't like the same things as they do.

2 _____ half of the class wants to work with computers in the future.

3 It's good to see you two bonding _____ each other so well.

4 It's quite uncommon _____ people to speak Russian in this country.

5 Jill settled _____ very quickly to her new life.

6 I thought you were my friend! You're supposed to stick _____ for me.

7 The majority _____ school leavers go on to university.

☐ **6**

b Complete the sentences with the correct form of *say* or *tell*.

1 Have you ever _told_ a joke where no one laughed?

2 She never _____ goodbye when she leaves the house.

3 I can't _____ the difference between one computer and another.

4 I crashed my bike into the wall and my dad really _____ me off.

5 It's no good _____ sorry now – it's too late.

6 He didn't even _____ thank you for the present.

☐ **5**

c Read clues 1–7 and fill in the puzzle with words about to work. What's the mystery word?

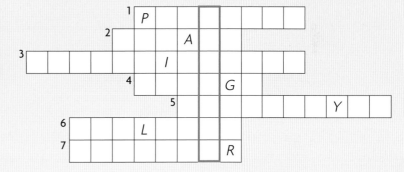

1 Work for only some of the week (2 words)
2 Money you get every month when you work
3 A degree certificate is an example of this
4 You decide to leave a job
5 When you haven't got a job
6 Person who works in a company
7 Person or company that gives you a job

☐ **7**

How did you do?

Tick (✓) a box for each section.

Total score: ☐ 51	☺ Very good	😐 OK	☹ Not very good
Grammar	26 – 33	17 – 25	less than 17
Vocabulary	15 – 18	9 – 14	less than 9

Module 2
Survival

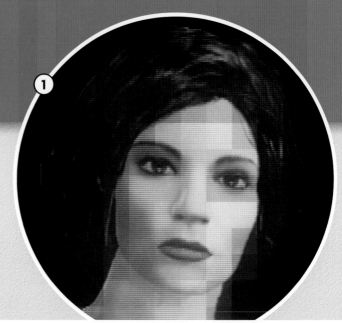

YOU WILL LEARN ABOUT ...

- A famous sailor ....
- A space tourist ....
- Intelligent computers ....
- The secrets of living a long life ....
- Tribes in danger ....
- Reality TV ....

 Can you match each picture with a topic?

YOU WILL LEARN HOW TO ...

Speak
- Discuss solo sailing
- Discuss space tourism
- Discuss amazing journeys
- Talk about holidays
- Discuss micro-chips in your brain
- Talk about the causes of stress
- Discuss organisations which help tribal people
- Talk about life in the future
- Discuss reality TV programmes
- Talk about rules in your home

Write
- An email about a trip
- A composition: life in the future
- A letter to a newspaper editor about plans to build a new hotel
- A magazine article about a new TV show

Read
- An article about a solo sailor
- An article about space tourism
- Short texts about famous travellers
- An article about artificial intelligence
- An article about an organisation that helps tribes
- An extract from a crime story
- An article about reality TV programmes

Listen
- An interview about a sailing project
- A radio programme about the secrets of long life
- Speeches about town development
- A radio interview about the negative side of reality TV
- A song

Use grammar

Can you match the names of the grammar points with the examples?

Future plans and arrangements	We won't win **unless** Andy plays.
Future predictions	The exam results **will be announced** next week.
First conditional with *if* and *unless*	You **mustn't** talk in here.
Present perfect passive	Alison's **had her hair cut**.
Future passive	Steve **might be** there, but Sally **probably won't be**.
Causative *have* (*have something done*)	**I'm going to see** the match tomorrow.
make / let / be allowed to	Oh no! My bike's **been stolen**!
Modal verbs for obligation, prohibition and permission	My parents **let** me drive their car.

Use vocabulary

Can you think of two more examples for each topic?

Travel	Television	Expressions with *make* and *do*	Extreme adjectives
journey	viewers	make sense	hungry → starving
timetable	presenter	do good	cold → freezing
....	....	....	....
....	....	....	....

(5) Travel

* Future review
* Vocabulary: travel
* Vocabulary: movement

1 Read and listen

(a) Look at the pictures. Do you know anything about this woman? Why do you think she is famous?

(b) Read the article quickly and answer the questions.

1 When did she become really famous, and why?

2 How long has she trained herself to sleep for?

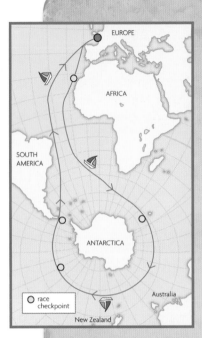

Britain's Solo Sailor

Ellen MacArthur started sailing when she was eight, going out on sailing trips with her aunt. She loved it so much that she saved her money for three years to buy her first small sailing boat. When she was 18, she sailed alone around Britain and won the 'Young Sailor of the Year' award.

But Ellen really became famous in 2001. Aged only 24, she was one of only two women who entered the Vendée Globe round the world solo race, which lasts 100 days. Despite many problems, she came second in the race out of 24 competitors and she was given a heroine's welcome when she returned.

Ambition and determination have always been a big part of Ellen's personality. When she was younger, she lived in a kind of hut for three years while she was trying to get sponsorship to compete in a transatlantic race. Then she took a one-way ticket to France, bought a tiny seven metre Classe Mini yacht, slept under it while she was repairing it, and then she raced it 4,000 kilometres across the Atlantic in 1997, alone for 33 days.

Ellen has had to learn many things, because sailing single-handed means that she has to be her own captain, electrician, sailmaker, engineer, doctor, journalist, cameraman and cook. She also has to be very fit, and because of the dangers of sleeping for long periods of time when she's in the middle of the ocean, she has trained herself to sleep for about 20 minutes at a time.

And she needs courage. Once, in the middle of the ocean, she had to climb the mast of her boat to repair the sails – at four o'clock in the morning, and with 100 kph winds blowing around her. It took her many hours to make the repairs; Ellen says: 'I was exhausted when I came down. It's hard to describe how it feels to be up there. It's like trying to hold onto a big pole, which for me is just too big to get my arms around, with someone kicking you all the time and trying to shake you off.'

But in her diary, Ellen also describes moments which make it all worthwhile: 'A beautiful sunrise started the day, with black clouds slowly lit by the bright yellow sun. I have a very strong feeling of pleasure, being out here on the ocean and having the chance to live this. I just feel lucky to be here.'

(c) 🔊 Read the text again and listen. Answer the questions.

1 When did she sail alone around Britain?

2 How many days is the *Vendée Globe* race?

3 Where did she live for three years, and why?

4 Where did she sleep when she was fixing the seven metre boat?

5 Why does she have to be her own electrician, sailmaker, etc.?

6 Why does she only sleep for about twenty minutes at a time?

Discussion box

Work in pairs or small groups. Discuss these questions together.

1 What do you think of Ellen MacArthur and what she does?

2 Could you do the things that she does? Why / Why not?

2 Listen

a 🔊 Listen to the interview with Ellen MacArthur in April 2003. She's talking about a new boat – a trimaran. Make notes about:

- the boat's size
- when it will be finished
- where they are building it

b 🔊 Listen again and answer the questions.

1 Why are trimarans usually 20 metres long?
2 What does Ellen want to do in the new boat?
3 What is 'the most important part of the design process'?
4 How long will it take to build the boat?
5 Why are they building it in Australia?
6 How will they bring the boat back to Britain?

3 Grammar

Future review

a Here are the three most common ways of talking about the future in English:

- *(be) going to*
  We use this to talk about decisions, plans and intentions made before the time of speaking.
  *We **aren't going to** use the new boat for races.*
  We also use it to predict the future when we can see something is starting to happen.
  *Look out! He's **going to** hit you!*

- present continuous
  We use this to talk about arrangements for the future.
  *They're **starting** in four weeks' time.*

- *will/won't (will not)*
  We use this to make predictions, offers and promises and for decisions made at the time of speaking.
  *It **will** be finished in December.*

b Look at the pictures and (circle) the correct words.

1 *We'll have / We're going to have* a party next Saturday – do you want to come?
2 The sky's getting darker – I think *it's raining / it's going to rain.*
3 It's possible that in 50 years there *won't be / aren't going to be* any tigers in the world.
4 *I won't study / I'm not going to study* medicine – I want to be an actor now.
5 I've got an appointment with the doctor – *I'm seeing / I'll see* her at 10 o'clock tomorrow.
6 People say that in 2020, computers *will be / are being* really small.

c Complete the sentences with the correct future form. Use the word at the end to help you.

1 I've got a date with Phil tonight – I .... (meet) him at 8 o'clock. *arrangement*
2 I've missed my bus, so I .... (walk) home. *intention*
3 In 2099, it .... (be) impossible to tell the difference between people and robots. *prediction*
4 I think Ellen MacArthur .... (break) more sailing records in the next few years. *prediction*
5 My parents .... (visit) my uncle and aunt next weekend. *arrangement*
6 My friend Megan .... (study) languages at university when she leaves school. *intention*

4 Pronunciation

/gənə/ *going to*

🔊 Turn to page 120.

5 Read

(a) Look at the photos. Who do you think the man is? Where do you think he is from? What do you think he is doing?

(b) Read the text quickly. What is the main subject of the text?

1 Dennis Tito is a hero because he flew into space when he was 60.
2 For the first time in history, a tourist made a trip into space.
3 The first tourist in space was sick when he drank a glass of fruit juice.

Space Tourists

Saturday 28 April, 2001: Dennis Tito was setting off on his holiday. 'So what?' you might think. Well, Mr Tito's journey was certainly unusual! So was the transport he chose, and the price of his trip.

The 60-year-old multi-millionaire from New York was sitting on board a Russian spaceship. He was on a journey to the International Space Station. It might have been a routine trip for the two cosmonauts who were travelling with him, but for him it was certainly no ordinary journey. Dennis Tito was the first tourist ever in space, and he had paid the sum of $20 million to go there. As the spacecraft left the earth's atmosphere, Tito drank a glass of fruit juice to celebrate and looked down at the earth's blue-green surface. Two minutes later, he was sick. Luckily it was only a minor problem. He soon recovered, and from then on enjoyed a smooth journey. When he arrived at the space station, there was a big smile on his face. 'A great trip!' he commented. 'I love space.'

For a long time space travel was something for heroes. But if some people are right, all this is going to change. One of them is Charles Miller, Director of a company called ProSpace. They are investing large amounts of money in space travel. 'Tito's adventure was just the beginning. We're going to see exciting new things in the next twenty years!' Charles Miller says.

Companies like ProSpace want space and space travel to belong to the public, not just governments. There are other plans, like cruises through space from one side of the world to the other. Maybe we will be able to depart from New York at nine o'clock in the morning, and arrive an hour later – in Tokyo! Such a schedule would allow the business traveller to return to New York on the same day, and still have eight hours for a meeting! How's that for speed?

(c) Read the text again. Underline the word that means:

1 starting a journey (paragraph 1)
2 normal (paragraph 2)
3 Russian astronauts (paragraph 2)
4 an amount of money (paragraph 2)
5 got better (paragraph 2)
6 said (paragraph 2)
7 leave (paragraph 3)

Discussion box

Work in pairs or small groups. Discuss these questions together.

1 Do you think that $20 million for the trip is too much?
2 Do you think that space tourism will be successful? Why / Why not?
3 Would you go on a holiday in space? Why / Why not?

6 Vocabulary

Travel

(a) Work with a partner. Discuss where you would find these things.

> terminal   customs   check-in desk   boarding card   platform
> departure lounge   timetable

(b) Circle the correct words.

1 When you go on a *cruise / flight / journey*, you spend your holiday on a large ship.

2 When you take a *cruise / flight / tour*, you travel by plane.

3 When you make a *journey / tour / cruise*, you travel from one place to another.

4 When you go on a *cruise / trip / tour*, you visit a place, usually for business or pleasure.

5 When you go on a *journey / flight / tour*, you travel for pleasure and visit several towns or places.

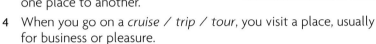

Look

We say
*get **on** a plane/train/bus/bike*
but
*get **in** a car/taxi*

(c) Complete the sentences. Use the correct form of the verbs in the box.

> miss   arrive in   check in   get in   arrive at   get on   take off

> The journey to the airport was horrible! The car wouldn't start, so we had to ¹_____ a taxi. We ²_____ the airport quite late. We ³_____ and they gave us our boarding cards. Then we ran through the terminal to the departure lounge, where everyone was waiting to ⁴_____ the plane.
>
> Suddenly, I remembered that I had left my passport at the check-in desk so I ran to get it. When I returned, the plane ⁵_____ ! So we ⁶_____ the flight.
>
> Luckily there was another plane two hours later, so we finally ⁷_____ Tokyo last night!

7 Speak

Work with a partner and read the situation. Imagine what will happen. Talk about it and use as many travel words from Exercise 6 as possible.

A British businessman is in a taxi, on his way to Heathrow airport in London. He is going to an important meeting in New York. The trip is extremely important, as he will lose £10,000 if he doesn't get to the meeting on time. He has left his passport at home, but he hasn't noticed this yet.

Culture in mind

8 Read

(a) Look at the four photos. What do you think the people did?

(b) Read the headings in the text and match the names to the pictures.

Going it Alone

Some travellers like to do things alone – here is a small selection of adventurers who did it solo.

Quimby flies the English Channel, 1912

Harriet Quimby was the first woman to get a pilot's licence in the USA, in August 1911. In 1912, she went to London and persuaded a newspaper to sponsor her to fly solo across the English Channel. Harriet took off from Dover at 5.30 am, and headed for France. She touched down in Calais, 40 kilometres away, where a cheering crowd met her. She went back to the USA and became America's First Lady of the Air – but tragically, she was killed in a flying accident in Boston, USA only ten weeks later, in July 1912.

Chichester sails alone round the world, 1967

Francis Chichester was 65 years old when he set off to sail around the world from Plymouth, England on 27 August, 1966 in his 80 metre boat *Gipsy Moth IV*. He stopped only once, for a few days in Sydney. He sailed 47,000 kilometres alone, returning to Plymouth 226 days later to a hero's welcome.

It was not his first solo achievement. In 1929, Chichester made the second solo flight from Britain to Australia, and in 1960 he won the first solo transatlantic race in *Gipsy Moth III*, by sailing from Plymouth to New York City in 40 days.

Riddles crosses Alaska, 1985

On Wednesday 20 March, 1985, American woman Libby Riddles made history by becoming the first woman to win the 1,700 kilometre Iditarod Sled Dog Race in Alaska. The race goes from Anchorage to the Bering Sea. Her feat captured the attention of the nation and she was named the 1985 Sportswoman of the Year by the Women's Sports Foundation and was given an award for her humane treatment of her dogs. Also, her dogs, Dugan and Sister, won the 1985 *Golden Harness* award, which is given to the best dogs during the Iditarod race.

Hempleman-Adams walks to the North Pole, 2003

In April 2003, David Hempleman-Adams became the first person to walk solo to the geomagnetic North Pole. The 500 kilometre journey took just under three weeks, and it involved pulling more than 45 kilos of equipment and supplies. It was his second attempt to walk to the North Pole. He said that at times the expedition had got extremely difficult and he had thought about giving up.

When he left home, he told his wife that he was going on a skiing holiday. She only learned the truth when he called her the day after finishing his journey.

c Read the text again and answer the questions.

1 Where did Francis Chichester stop on his voyage?
2 When and how was Harriet Quimby killed?
3 What did David Hempleman-Adams tell his wife before he started his walk to the North Pole?
4 Who won awards in the Iditarod race in Alaska, apart from Libby Riddles?
5 Which journey was the longest in time? Which was the shortest in distance?

Discussion box

Work in pairs or small groups. Discuss these questions together.

1 Which of the four journeys do you think was the most amazing? Why?
2 Imagine you could do a solo journey. Where would you go to/from?

9 Vocabulary

Movement

a Look at the paragraph about Harriet Quimby in Exercise 8b. Replace the underlined words with words from the text.

1 Harriet started her flight from Dover.
2 She went in the direction of France.
3 She landed in Calais.
4 She returned to the USA.

b Complete the sentences. Use the words you found in the Quimby text in the correct form.

1 He got in his car and _____ London.
2 Their plane _____ half an hour ago, so they should be flying over the sea by now.
3 I forgot my bag so I _____ to get it.
4 The spaceship _____ at Cape Canaveral.

10 Write

a Read Hannah's email to a friend. How long is she staying in Barcelona?

b When we write emails, we often use a very informal style. For example:

1 Hannah doesn't always use a personal pronoun in certain sentences: *Arrived here yesterday ...* Find four more examples of this.
2 She uses an emoticon. Can you find it? What does it mean? Do you know any others?
3 How does Hannah start and finish her message?

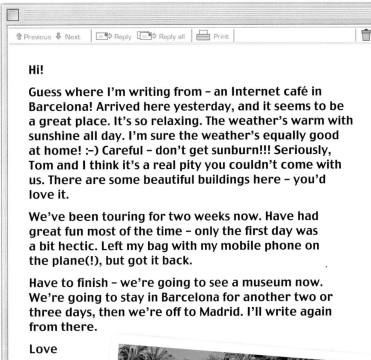

⇧ Previous ⇩ Next   Reply   Reply all   Print 🗑

Hi!

Guess where I'm writing from – an Internet café in Barcelona! Arrived here yesterday, and it seems to be a great place. It's so relaxing. The weather's warm with sunshine all day. I'm sure the weather's equally good at home! :-) Careful – don't get sunburn!!! Seriously, Tom and I think it's a real pity you couldn't come with us. There are some beautiful buildings here – you'd love it.

We've been touring for two weeks now. Have had great fun most of the time – only the first day was a bit hectic. Left my bag with my mobile phone on the plane(!), but got it back.

Have to finish – we're going to see a museum now. We're going to stay in Barcelona for another two or three days, then we're off to Madrid. I'll write again from there.

Love

Hannah

c Imagine that either Ellen MacArthur or Dennis Tito is writing to a friend while travelling. Write her/his email, using Hannah's email to help you. Write 120–150 words. Write about:

- where you are on your trip
- anything special that happened recently
- what you can see outside
- how you are feeling
- when you'll write again

6 Live forever!

* Future predictions
* First conditional review, *if* and *unless*
* Vocabulary: verbs with prepositions
* Vocabulary: phrasal verbs with *into*

THE AGE OF Intelligent Machines RAYMOND KURZWEIL

1 Read and listen

a Ray Kurzweil works with computers. Which of these things do you think he does?

1 writes books
2 composes music
3 teaches languages
4 designs games
5 helps people who have disabilities
6 does research

b 🔊 Read the text and listen to check your ideas.

c Match the titles A–E with the paragraphs. Write A–E in the spaces.

A A new pair of ears
B An author and researcher
C Electronic immortality
D Computers that speak
E A new pair of eyes

Discussion box

Work in pairs or small groups. Discuss these questions together.

1 Which computer chips would you like to have in your brain? Choose from these or think of your own.
   more memory
   foreign language
   increase your confidence

2 Do you like the idea of living forever in a computer? Why / Why not?

INTELLIGENT MACHINES

1 ⬜ Medical scientists are already putting computer chips directly into the brain to help people who have Parkinson's disease, but in what other ways might computer technology be able to help us? Ray Kurzweil is author of the successful book *The Age of Intelligent Machines* and is one of the world's best computer research scientists. He is researching the possibilities.

2 ⬜ Kurzweil gets computers to recognise voices. An example of this is Ramona, the virtual hostess of Kurzweil's homepage, who is programmed to understand what you say. Visitors to the site can have their own conversations with her, and Ramona also dances and sings.

3 ⬜ Kurzweil uses this technology to help people with physical disabilities. One of his ideas is a 'seeing machine'. This will be 'like a friend that could describe what is going on in the visible world', he explains. Blind people will use a visual sensor which will probably be built into a pair of sunglasses. This sensor will describe to the person everything it sees.

4 ⬜ Another idea, which is likely to help deaf people, is the 'listening machine'. This invention will recognise millions of words and understand any speaker. The listening machine will also be able to translate into other languages, so even people without hearing problems are likely to be interested in using it.

5 ⬜ But it is not just about helping people with disabilities. Looking further into the future, Kurzweil sees a time when we will be able to download our entire consciousness onto a computer. This technology probably won't be ready for at least 50 years, but when it arrives, it means our minds will be able to live forever.

2 Grammar

Future predictions

a Use the text in Exercise 1 to complete these sentences.

1 In what other ways .... computer technology be able to help us?

2 Blind people .... use a visual sensor which .... be built into a pair of sunglasses.

3 People without hearing problems .... be interested in using the listening machine.

4 This technology .... be ready for at least 50 years.

b Complete the chart with the words in the box.

~~will~~   will probably   ~~isn't likely to~~   won't   might not
probably won't   is likely to   ~~might~~

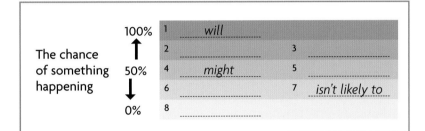

The chance of something happening	100% ↑ 50% ↓ 0%	1 _will_		
		2	3	
		4 _might_	5	
		6	7 _isn't likely to_	
		8		

c Decide if the speaker in these situations is sure or not sure. Complete the sentences with *'ll*, *won't*, *might* or *might not*.

1 A: 'I _'m going to_ Disneyland in Paris next week.'

   B: 'Oh, you .... love it. I went there last year and it was wonderful.'

2 A: 'Are you coming to the party tonight?'

   B: 'Actually, I .... I want to, but I have to get up early tomorrow. Ask me again later.'

3 A: 'Do you know where you're going for your holidays next year?'

   B: 'We .... go to South Africa. We haven't really decided yet, though.'

4 A: 'Can I have the last piece of pizza?'

   B: 'If you do, there .... be any left for your brother!'

d Rewrite the sentences, using the word in brackets.

1 She's always late so she's not likely to arrive before nine. **(probably)**

   She probably won't arrive before nine.

2 He'll get to the tennis final but he probably won't win. **(likely)**

3 Tomorrow's a holiday so the traffic is likely to be bad. **(probably)**

4 He hasn't studied at all so he'll probably fail the test. **(likely)**

5 The weather forecast says it's not likely to rain tomorrow. **(probably)**

e Work with a partner and make predictions about these subjects.

1 Dinosaurs will be brought back to life.
   A: *That isn't likely to happen.*   B: *I think it might happen.*

2 Men will give birth to babies.

3 Your country will win the next World Cup.

4 We'll discover life on other planets.

5 You'll pass the end-of-year exams.

6 You'll get married before you're 20.

7 You'll find the perfect partner.

8 You'll have four or more children.

3 Listen

(a) How old is the oldest person you know?

(b) Look at the list of items in the box, and say which things you think help people to live longer, and which things don't help. Explain why to a partner.

> smoking and drinking   stress
> sitting in the sun
> eating lettuce at night
> going to bed early   having fun
> doing exercise   singing
> not eating meat
> taking vitamins   getting angry
> doing crosswords

(c) 🔊 Listen to part of a programme with various people talking about what they think will help them to live longer. Tick (✓) the items in the box which are mentioned.

(d) 🔊 Listen to the second part of the programme, and choose answer a, b or c.

1. The presenter says that the secret to living longer is:
   a to live in a cold country   b genetic
   c taking care of our bodies
2. Kari Steffanson says that Icelandic people:
   a want to know about nature
   b are very interested in their ancestors
   c love record-collecting
3. They did research on people who died:
   a at different ages   b between 1970 and 1990
   c in Viking times
4. The people who lived longer:
   a had a healthier life   b liked each other more
   c were usually from the same family
5. She says that people from Iceland have similar lifestyles because:
   a they are so healthy   b it is a small country
   c they are all related
6. The researchers will make new drugs from the different gene they discovered if:
   a they live long enough   b they get permission
   c they find out how it works

4 Grammar
First conditional review, *if* and *unless*

(a) Circle the correct words in the sentences from the radio programme.

1. I think that unless *I do / will do* some exercise, I *don't live / won't live* very long.
2. If *you'll do / you do* all those things, *you'll live / you live* as long as me.

(b) Circle the correct words.

> **Rule:**
> - In these sentences, both verbs refer to actions or events in the *present / future*.
> - The verb tense after the words **if** or **unless** is *present simple / will or won't*.
> - The verb tense in the other clause is *present simple / will or won't*.

(c) Complete the sentences with the verbs in the box.

> 'll copy   come   leave   'll help
> won't call   ~~'ll fall~~   won't get
> aren't   want   want

1. You *'ll fall* if you _____ careful.
2. If you _____ shopping with me now, I _____ you with your homework later.
3. Unless we _____ the house right now, we _____ there for the start of the film.
4. I _____ this CD for you if you _____.
5. I _____ you at the weekend – unless you _____ me to.

(d) Make sentences from these words. Use *if* or *unless*.

1. you play with matches / burn your fingers
2. bite you / you go near that dog
3. come and eat your pizza now / not be any left
4. you are tired / I do the washing up
5. you slow down / you crash the car
6. buy you a new bike / pass all your exams

Time conjunctions: *if / unless / when / until / as soon as*

e Match the two parts of the sentences.

1	As soon as I arrive at the station,	a	he'll probably need glasses.
2	Unless I work faster,	b	until she says sorry.
3	When he gets old,	c	you won't get wet.
4	If you take an umbrella,	d	I won't finish on time.
5	I won't speak to her	e	I'll ring you.

f (Circle) the correct words.

1 A: We'll be here all night *when* / *unless* you do something.

   B: There's nothing I can do. We'll stay here *until* / *if* someone rescues us.

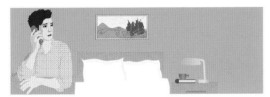

2 A: Someone's downstairs! I'm afraid something will happen to me *until* / *if* you don't come soon.

   B: Alright. I'll come round. And phone the police *until* / *as soon as* we finish talking, OK?

3 A: I want to keep it a secret. *If* / *As soon as* you see Joey, don't tell him anything.

   B: OK, I won't say anything *unless* / *as soon as* you tell me to.

4 A: Have you heard? Sarah's going to leave her boyfriend *as soon as* / *until* he gets back from holiday.

   B: No way! He's going to be so upset *when* / *if* he finds out.

5 Vocabulary and speaking
Verbs with prepositions

a Here are some common causes of stress. Complete them, using the prepositions in the box.

with	for	about

1 arguing .... your parents
2 revising .... exams
3 getting ready .... school
4 thinking .... what to wear
5 worrying .... life

b Complete each sentence. Use a verb + preposition from Exercise 5a.

1 I'm going to have a shower and get dressed, to .... the party.
2 I got into real trouble at school yesterday. Perhaps it wasn't a good idea to .... the teacher!
3 She's always happy and smiling – she never seems to .... anything!
4 Sorry, I can't some out tonight. There's a test tomorrow and I need to .... it.
5 It's time to plan the party. We need to .... who to invite!

c Work with a partner. Discuss how stressful the things in Exercise 5a are. Give each one a mark from 0 (not at all) to 5 (extremely). What other things make you stressed?

d In groups of four, compare what you find most stressful in life and give each other ideas on how to make these things less stressful.

6 Pronunciation
Weak and strong forms of prepositions

🔊 Turn to page 120.

Ben calls Caroline

7 Read and listen

a 🔊 What do Caroline and Ben think about Joanne? Why is Caroline worried about Matt? Read, listen and check your answers.

Caroline: Hello?

Ben: Hi – Caroline? It's Ben.

Caroline: Ben? Hey, this is a surprise. I thought you were in Hong Kong.

Ben: Well, I was – I came back a week or so ago, with my mum.

Caroline: Is your dad still there?

Ben: Yeah, my parents broke up some time ago – but listen, Caroline, I don't want to go into all that right now, if that's OK. Tell me, how're things with you?

Caroline: Yeah, not too bad, thanks – but what made you think to call me?

Ben: Well, believe it or not, I bumped into Matt this morning, and he mentioned you. So I thought I'd give you a ring.

Caroline: That's nice. Funnily enough, I was thinking about Matt the other day too.

Ben: Oh yeah? And Caroline – guess what? Matt's going out with Joanne Willis now.

Caroline: Yes, I know.

Ben: She was always a bit full of herself, as I remember. Between you and me, I think Matt's crazy to be going out with her.

Caroline: Oh, come on, Ben, give people a chance. I know Joanne used to be a bit difficult, but she's turned into a really nice person now. In fact, we're pretty good friends.

Ben: Really? I'm sorry, Caroline, I didn't mean to—

Caroline: It's OK, Ben. Listen, did Matt mention the party tomorrow evening?

Ben: Yes, he did, actually. I'm thinking of going along. He said you were going, too.

Caroline: Yeah, I'll probably go – although Matt'll play all that indie music.

Ben: Yeah, I know what you mean, it isn't my favourite either. But it'll be great to see you again, you know, catch up on things.

Caroline: It'll be good to see you again, Ben. But the real reason I'm going is because I'm a bit worried about Matt.

Ben: Really? Why?

Caroline: Well, the fact is, Joanne told me he's in a bit of trouble – something to do with money.

Ben: Oh? That's funny, he didn't say anything to me about any trouble.

Caroline: Well, he wouldn't, would he? After all, he hasn't seen you for a year or so. Look, Ben, I've got to go. See you tomorrow at Matt's place?

Ben: Absolutely. I'll see you there, Caroline. Take care.

Caroline: Bye, Ben – and thanks for calling.

b Mark the statements *T* (true) or *F* (false). Correct the false statements.

1 Caroline is surprised that Ben has phoned her. ☐

2 Ben wants to talk about his parents breaking up. ☐

3 Ben thinks Matt is lucky to have Joanne as his girlfriend. ☐

4 Ben is looking forward to meeting Caroline at the party. ☐

5 Caroline thinks it is strange that Matt didn't tell Ben about his problem. ☐

8 Everyday English

a Find expressions 1–4 in the story. Who says them?

1 believe it or not   2 between you and me
3 I know what you mean   4 the fact is

Which one is used:

a before saying what you think is the most important thing? ☐

b before saying something you think is very surprising? ☐

c before saying something you don't want the other person to repeat to anyone else? ☐

d to say that you understand the other person's idea? ☐

b Complete the sentences with an expression from Exercise 8a.

1 I asked her to do all my homework for me for a month – and ...., she agreed!

2 I'm sorry, I can't talk to you right now. ...., my mother's in hospital and I need to get there.

3 **A:** James cooked a special dinner for me last night, but ...., it was awful!
   B: Oh, ... – James is a terrible cook!

9 Vocabulary

Phrasal verbs with *into*

a Match the underlined verbs with the meanings.

1 I bumped into Matt the other day. ☐
2 I don't want to go into all that right now. ☐
3 She's turned into a really nice person. ☐
4 The police are looking into the death of an old man. ☐

a talk about
b become
c meet by chance, accident
d investigate

b Complete each sentence with one of the phrasal verbs above, in the correct form.

1 It was a really scary film – especially when that guy .... a green giant!

2 There's a smell of gas in the kitchen. I think we should .... it.

3 He's a horrible person. I hope I never .... him again!

4 I don't want to .... all the details about why I failed the exam.

10 Write

a Look at the title of the composition. Does the writer agree or disagree? Read the text quickly to find out.

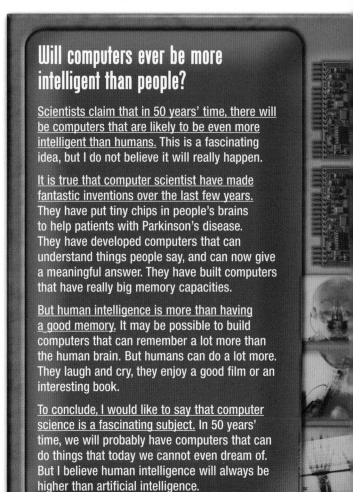

Will computers ever be more intelligent than people?

Scientists claim that in 50 years' time, there will be computers that are likely to be even more intelligent than humans. This is a fascinating idea, but I do not believe it will really happen.

It is true that computer scientist have made fantastic inventions over the last few years. They have put tiny chips in people's brains to help patients with Parkinson's disease. They have developed computers that can understand things people say, and can now give a meaningful answer. They have built computers that have really big memory capacities.

But human intelligence is more than having a good memory. It may be possible to build computers that can remember a lot more than the human brain. But humans can do a lot more. They laugh and cry, they enjoy a good film or an interesting book.

To conclude, I would like to say that computer science is a fascinating subject. In 50 years' time, we will probably have computers that can do things that today we cannot even dream of. But I believe human intelligence will always be higher than artificial intelligence.

b Read the composition again. Which paragraph(s):

1 develop the writer's ideas?
2 sum up the writer's main ideas?
3 say what they are writing about?

c Write your own composition about one of the following topics. Use the composition on computers to help you. Write 120–150 words. Each paragraph should have a topic sentence, where you give the main idea, and a few more sentences to support or explain your ideas. In the composition above, the topic sentences have been underlined.

- Will there still be schools and teachers in the future?

- Will it be possible to live forever?

For your portfolio

7 Campaigning for survival

* Present passive and past passive review
* Present perfect passive and future passive
* Causative *have* (*have something done*)
* Vocabulary: *make* and *do*

1 Read and listen

a Look at the pictures and answer the questions.

1 Where do you think the person is from?
2 What kind of life do you think they have?

b Read the text quickly to check your ideas.

c Match the titles A–D with the paragraphs. Write A–D in the spaces.

A The effects of forced settlement on tribes
B The Jarawa's lifestyle
C A successful fight
D Who the Jarawa are

d 🔊 Read the text again and listen. Answer the questions.

1 Why is very little known about the Jarawa?
2 What possible results can forced settlement have on tribes?
3 Why did the Indian government give up their plans to settle the Jarawa's land?
4 How has *Survival* been successful in helping the Jarawa?

Discussion box

Work in pairs or small groups. Discuss these questions together.

1 How would you feel if you were told to live in a different place?
2 Would you support an organisation like *Survival*? Why / Why not?

Tribes In Danger

Survival

Survival is an international organisation which helps endangered tribes. It was founded in 1969, and today has supporters in 82 countries. Here is one of the success stories.

1 ☐ The Jarawa are a tribe of 200–300 people, and they live on the Andaman Islands in the Indian Ocean. They look very different from their Indian neighbours. Most probably, their closest relatives are African. No one outside the tribe really speaks their language, and so not much is known about them.

2 ☐ But we do know how the Jarawa live. They are nomadic people, moving from place to place to find food. They hunt small animals and fish, they find berries, honey, and they are self-sufficient – they do everything themselves.

3 ☐ The threats to the Jarawa started in 1970. A road was built through the forest where they live, and the Indian authorities decided to build towns and 'settlers' were brought from other places to live in them. They also wanted the Jarawa to live in the towns. This policy is called 'forced settlement', and it has been a disaster for tribal peoples in places all over the world. It's clear why: because of forced settlement, tribes are no longer self-sufficient, and they can easily get new diseases. A tribe's sense of identity can easily be destroyed.

4 ☐ But in the case of the Jarawa, it seems that the fight against these dangers has been successful, thanks to *Survival* and the campaigns that they've organised. For a number of years, *Survival* asked the Indian government to respect the Jarawa's rights to live on their land. As a result of the campaign, there was a court case and eventually the authorities closed the road through the Jarawa's land. They also had the settlers removed. Now *Survival* is fighting for the Jarawa's right to own their land and to make their own choices about how they live.

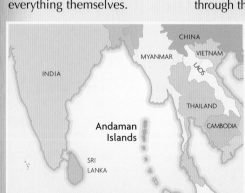

CHINA
MYANMAR
VIETNAM
LAOS
INDIA
THAILAND
CAMBODIA
Andaman Islands
SRI LANKA

2 Grammar

Present passive and past passive review

a Look at the sentences and write *present simple passive* or *past simple passive* in the spaces.

*Not much **is known** about the Jarawas.* ....

*A road **was built** through the forest.* ....

b Find more examples of the passive in the text in Exercise 1. Then complete the rule. Use *by*, *to be* and *past participle*.

> **Rule:**
> - We form the passive with a form of the verb .... and the ....
> - We use the preposition .... to say who or what does the action, but only if this is important.

c Complete the sentences with the correct form of the verbs.

1 *Survival* .... (support) by people in many parts of the world.

2 A few years ago, the 'Right Livelihood Award', known as the alternative Nobel Prize, ... (give) to *Survival*.

3 The President of *Survival* .... (interview) on TV six months ago.

4 *Survival* .... not .... (fund) by any government.

5 Last year, a number of unknown tribes .... (discover) in various parts of the world.

6 It's hard to believe how badly some tribes .... (treat) by governments.

7 Some time ago, a film .... (make) about the situation of tribal people worldwide.

8 A lot .... (know) about how diseases .... (bring) to tribal people.

3 Grammar

Causative *have* (*have something done*)

a Look at the examples.

*They also **had the settlers removed**.*

*I must go and **have my hair cut**.*

*My mum **had a new phone line installed** in her office.*

b In each sentence, who is the subject? Do we know who does the action?

c Complete the rule with *us* and *someone*.

> **Rule:**
> - We often use causative *have* when we arrange for .... to do something for .... (often as a service).

d Mr Hill never does anything himself. Complete the sentences with the correct form of causative *have*. Write three more sentences.

1 He never washes his car himself. He always has it …

2 He doesn't cut the grass in his garden. He …

3 He never makes his own breakfast. He …

'He always has his hair cut.'

e Make sentences that are true for you using *have (something) done* and the words from the box.

pierce/ears	dye/hair
shave/head	tattoo/body

- Many of my friends …
- None of my friends …
- My parents wouldn't allow me to …
- I would love to …
- I would hate to …
- My parents don't want me to …

4 Pronunciation

Stress pattern in *have something done*

🔊 Turn to page 120.

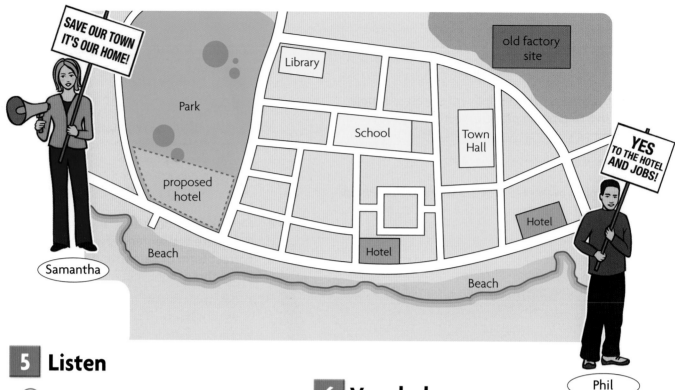

5 Listen

(a) Samantha and Phil are teenagers who live in a small town on the coast of Britain. There is a plan to build a new hotel in the town, on part of the park. Look at the pictures. Who likes the plan? Who doesn't like it?

(b) 🔊 Listen to Samantha talking to a crowd of people. Mark the statements *T* (true) or *F* (false). Correct the false statements.

1 Two hotels have been built in the town in the last year. ☐

2 She thinks the developers only want to make money. ☐

3 She thinks the hotel should be built in the town. ☐

4 She wants people to help to keep the town the way it is. ☐

(c) 🔊 Now listen to Phil talking to the crowd after Samantha. Complete these notes.

> Phil says that the town won't be
> ¹_____ if the new hotel is built. The
> new hotel will bring the town ²_____ .
> And the old factory site has been bought
> by ³_____ , who are going to build
> ⁴_____ on the land. More tourists
> will also mean ⁵_____ for the people
> who live in the town.

(d) Who do you agree with: Samantha or Phil?

6 Vocabulary

make and *do*

(a) 🔊 Here are some things that Samantha and Phil said. Complete the sentences with the correct form of *make* or *do*. Then listen again and check.

1 A lot of trees will be cut down to _____ room for the hotel.

2 The developers are going to _____ a mess of the town.

3 They're only interested in _____ money.

4 It doesn't _____ sense to build another hotel in the town.

5 Let's all _____ our best to keep this town a really nice place!

6 Let's all _____ a big effort to stop them destroying the town.

7 I don't want to _____ fun of Samantha.

8 We need to _____ progress here.

9 I think that a new hotel will _____ a big difference to the town.

10 This plan will _____ the town a lot of good.

(b) Put the phrases in the correct column. What other examples can you think of?

~~progress~~ your best	make	do
money fun of (someone)		
a difference sense	progress	
a lot of good an effort		
a mess room		

7 Grammar
Present perfect passive

a Complete the sentences with the verbs in the box. Then complete the rule.

> has been bought
> have been told
> have been built

1 Two hotels .... here in the last five years.
2 I know what we .... : 'Build a new hotel and more jobs will be created'.
3 The old factory site .... by other developers.

> **Rule:**
> - We form the present perfect passive with the present perfect form of the verb .... + the ....

b Complete the sentences with the correct form of the verbs. Use present perfect passive and past simple passive.

1 Since the beginning of the 20th century, a lot of new technology _has been developed_ . (develop)
2 In 1928, the first television pictures .... (send) from London to New York.
3 Since then, billions of TV sets .... (sell) all over the world.
4 In the 1970s, TV sets .... (give) to tribes in the Amazon.
5 But since then, special TV programmes .... (not developed) for the people in the tribes.
6 Many governments and authorities .... (criticise) for bringing TV into tribal cultures.

8 Grammar
Future passive

a Complete these sentences with the verbs in the box.

> will be built   will be cut   won't be destroyed

1 A lot of really nice trees in the park .... down.
2 The town .... by the new hotel.
3 A new sports centre .... on that land.

b Look at the sentences in Exercise 8a and complete the rule.

> **Rule:**
> - We form the future passive with .... or .... + be + the ....

c Complete the sentences with the correct form of the verbs.

New Bobby Moore Sports Centre

The town authorities have announced that a new sports centre [1] .... (build) over the next five years. The new sports centre [2] .... (name) after Bobby Moore, the captain of the England football team that won the World Cup in 1966.
A competition [3] .... (hold) for the design of the sports centre, but the name of the competition winner [4] .... (not announce) until the end of next year. The site for the new building [5] .... (choose) next month. After that, the decision about which company will actually build the sports centre [6] .... (make) by the town authorities.

9 Speak

Work with a partner and discuss the topics below. What things do you think will be done in each one in the future?

> space exploration   computers   your town   language learning

A: *I think life will be found on other planets.*
B: *Perhaps computer chips will be put inside our bodies.*

Fiction in mind

10 Read

(a) How many titles of thrillers do you know in English? Have you seen or read any of them? Which?

But Was it Murder?
by Jania Barrell

The story

Alex Forley had everything: good looks, money, a beautiful house in London, an attractive girlfriend and a close group of friends. But now he is dead and Detective Inspector Rod Eliot wants the answers to two simple questions. Was it murder? And if so, who was the murderer?

'Any developments?' asked Eliot.
'Well, sir, we've just heard that there were several people's fingerprints in the house. But on the gun, there were only the dead man's.'

5 'Not a great help,' said Eliot. 'It could still be suicide. Or an accident. Or murder. Maybe someone shot him, cleaned the gun, and then put it in his hand to look like suicide. Well, we'd better see Amanda Grant and take her to look at the body. Then we'll
10 make another visit to the Crowthers.'

Amanda Grant lived in Greenwich, which was halfway between New Cross and Blackheath. Eliot wanted to start early to avoid the crowds as much as possible.

★ ★ ★

15 'Good morning,' said Eliot. 'I'm Detective Inspector Eliot, and this is Detective Constable Bowen. We'd like to speak to Amanda Grant, if she's at home.'

'I'm Amanda Grant,' she answered. Her voice was unusually deep. 'What can I do for you, Inspector?'
20 'May we come in, Miss Grant?' asked Eliot. 'It would be easier to talk inside.' She looked surprised but calmly asked them to come in. The front door opened directly into a sitting room, where bright curtains and carpets gave a warm feeling. A cat was
25 washing itself on a chair. Through the window Eliot could see the yellow and white shapes of the Millennium Dome beside the river. In front of it a boat moved slowly towards the centre of Greenwich. Piano music was coming from a CD player next to a large

desk covered with papers and books. At one end a 30 single rose stood in a glass vase. Eliot felt very unwilling to bring the subject of death and guns into this peaceful room.

She did not say a word while he spoke, or for a long time afterwards. 35
'I suppose you'll want me to identify the body,' she said eventually. 'You obviously need to make sure it's Alex.' Her face showed no sign of what she was feeling.

Eliot wondered how many more strong and intelligent women they would find in Forley's life. 40
'Yes, I'm afraid so, Miss Grant,' he said. 'We'll take you there now, if you don't mind. After that, we'll need to ask you some questions.'

Her face was pale as she switched off the music and put on her coat. But she was quite calm as she got into 45 the car. Could she really be as cool as she seemed?

Eliot looked at her closely as they went into the building. She still showed no sign of strong feeling. Her hands started to shake only when the body was brought out and the plastic sheet taken off. Of course, 50 the head remained covered. If she could not be sure without seeing the face, they would have to use fingerprints and dentist's records. But he did not think this would be necessary. Anyone who knew this man would recognise those long fingers. She looked quickly 55 at the body, and nodded at Eliot.

'You're certain?' he had to ask.

She touched the man's right hand for a moment. Then she started to cry.

(b) Read the extract from the story. Answer the questions.

1 What did the police know about the man's death?
2 Inspector Eliot went to see Amanda at her home. Had he met her before? How do you know?
3 Why did the Inspector feel unwilling to talk about the man's death?
4 What did the Inspector think about the fact that Amanda didn't show any strong feelings for quite a long time?

Discussion box

Work in pairs or small groups.
Discuss these questions together.

1 Do you like reading crime stories?
Why / Why not?

2 What is the best crime story or film
you've read or seen? What did you
like about it?

11 Write

(a) Read Hilary Riley's letter to a newspaper.
Why is she writing? What is she worried
about?

(b) Read the letter again and answer the
questions.

1 What useful phrase does Hilary use to
state what she is worried about?

2 Underline the topic sentence in each
paragraph. How does she support the idea
expressed in the topic sentence?

3 What does she suggest in her conclusion?

(c) Imagine you are either Samantha or Phil in
Exercise 5a. Write her/his letter to the
editor of a newspaper about the hotel plan.
Use Hilary's letter to help you. Write 120–150
words. Follow this plan:

– In the first paragraph, state your reason for
writing.

– In the next few paragraphs, develop your
ideas. Remember to use topic sentences.

– To conclude, state what you think should
happen / should be done.

Dear Sir

I am writing to express my concern about the plans
to build a motorway near our village.

Haldersham is one of the loveliest villages in
England. It is peaceful and quiet, and it is situated
in a very attractive valley. There are also several
beautiful countryside walks in the surroundings.

Most of the people who live in Haldersham have
moved here from other places, often from London.
They have bought houses here to live in a place far
away from the noise and the stress of the big city.
They paid a lot of money for their houses, but they
knew they would get a high quality of life for it.

If the planned motorway is built, life in
Haldersham will change dramatically. There will
be a lot of noise, and nobody will want to go on
the walks. House prices will certainly go down,
because nobody will want to buy houses in a place
close to a motorway. Haldersham will become an
ugly place.

I don't think any of the residents of our beautiful
village want that. So, let's all tell the politicians
who support the motorway plans what we think
about them!

Yours faithfully

Hilary Riley

Hilary Riley

8 Reality TV

* *make / let / be allowed to*
* Modal verbs of obligation, prohibition and permission
* Vocabulary: television
* Vocabulary: extreme adjectives and modifiers
* Vocabulary: collocations with *on*

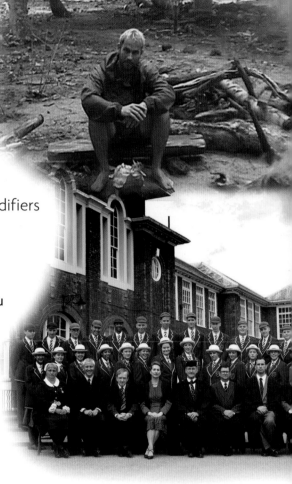

1 Read and listen

a Look at the pictures and the title of the text. What do you know about reality TV? Read the text quickly to check your ideas.

REALITY TV

Reality TV began in the early 1980s, when a Japanese television company made a series of programmes called *Endurance*. Starting with thousands of contestants in the first show, the programme presenters made them do really difficult and/or unpleasant things every episode. The presenters made fun of the contestants, too. Viewing figures in Japan were enormous.

In *Survivor*, sixteen people are taken to a remote island and made to stay there for more than a month. They have to find their own food or go hungry. The producers let the contestants take one luxury item each. Every three days, one contestant must leave the island and the last person wins £1 million.

It's not just adults who take part in these shows. A television series in Britain in 2003, called *That'll teach 'em*, took 30 teenagers and put them in a fictional King's school, where they lived for one month and received 1950s-style tuition. The pupils were made to wear thick 1950s school uniforms (including a school hat) during the hot summer and they had to do a long run every day. 'They made us have cold showers and we had to have our hands checked every day to see if they were clean,' says one pupil. 'We weren't allowed to take anything from our modern lives into the school'. Although there was no prize money in this programme, the teenagers learned a lot from the experience.

In 2004, there was a programme in Britain where contestants were not allowed to sleep for seven days to try to win £97,000 prize money. The winner was 19-year-old Clare Southern. *Shattered* had many complaints from viewers.

But where will it stop? Programmes like this are broadcast all over the world. But there are people who think that these programmes degrade both the contestants and the viewers, and feel that contestants are often made to do dangerous things to make good television.

b 🔊 Read again and listen. Mark the statements *T* (true) or *F* (false). Correct the false statements.

1 Reality TV programmes started more than 20 years ago in Japan. ☐

2 In *Survivor*, contestants are taken to an island and have to stay there for a month. ☐

3 The pupils were allowed to take mobile phones with them. ☐

4 The pupils won some money. ☐

5 The winner of *Shattered* was a teenager. ☐

6 *Shattered* was popular with everyone. ☐

Discussion box

Work in pairs or small groups. Discuss these questions together.

1 Would you like to be a contestant on a reality TV show? Why / Why not?

2 Would you like to go back in time to your parents' education system?

2 Grammar and speaking

make / let / be allowed to

a Look at these examples from the text.

*The producers **let the contestants take** one luxury item each.*

*The pupils **were made to wear** thick 1950s school uniforms.*

*They **made us have** cold showers.*

*The contestants **were not allowed to sleep** for seven days.*

b Find more examples of these structures in the text.

c (Circle) the correct option to complete the rules.

> **Rule:**
> - We use **be allowed to** to talk about *obligation / permission.*
> - We use **not be allowed to** to talk about *prohibition / obligation.*
> - We use **let** to talk about *obligation / permission.*
> - We use **make** to talk about *obligation / permission.*

d Look at the two examples with *make* in Exercise 2a.

1 Which one is *active*, and which one is *passive*?

2 What is different about the verbs that follow *make* in these examples?

e Complete the sentences with the correct form of *make*, *let* or *be allowed to*.

1 At school, we (not) .... take our mobile phones into the classroom.

2 .... your teachers .... you study hard?

3 I never .... people use my things without asking me first.

4 When I lend things to my brother, I always .... him promise to be careful!

5 .... you .... use your mum's car?

6 I .... usually .... come home later at the weekend.

7 Joanna's bought a new CD, and yesterday she .... me borrow it.

8 Last Saturday, my parents .... me go shopping with them – it was really boring!

f Work in pairs. Ask and answer questions about the rules you have at home. Talk about:

> homework   times you can come home
> doing housework   listening to music in your room
> friends visiting you   using the phone

A: *Are you allowed to listen to music in your room?*

B: *Yeah, but after 11 o'clock at night they make me use headphones. Do your parents make you ...?*

3 Vocabulary

Television

a Complete the text with the words in the box.

> series   contestant   celebrities
> presenter   viewing figures   episode
> audience   viewers   sitcoms

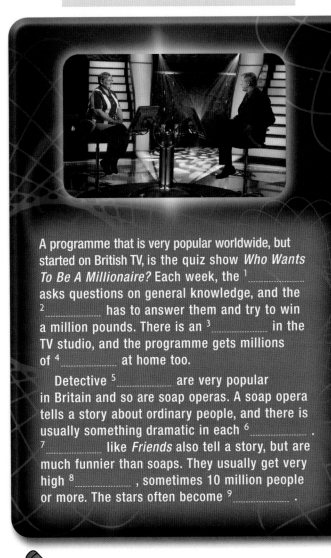

A programme that is very popular worldwide, but started on British TV, is the quiz show *Who Wants To Be A Millionaire?* Each week, the [1] .... asks questions on general knowledge, and the [2] .... has to answer them and try to win a million pounds. There is an [3] .... in the TV studio, and the programme gets millions of [4] .... at home too.

Detective [5] .... are very popular in Britain and so are soap operas. A soap opera tells a story about ordinary people, and there is usually something dramatic in each [6] .... [7] .... like *Friends* also tell a story, but are much funnier than soaps. They usually get very high [8] .... , sometimes 10 million people or more. The stars often become [9] ....

Look

- *viewers* watch a programme on television.
- *an audience* watches a film in a cinema, a play in a theatre, or a programme being made in a TV studio.
- *spectators* are people who go to watch a sporting event.

4 Pronunciation

/aʊ/ *allowed*

◁)) Turn to page 120.

5 Listen

(a) You are going to listen to an interview with a psychologist about reality TV. Look at the questions asked by the interviewer. Work with a partner and make sure you understand what they mean.

1 Don't these programmes put people under enormous pressure?

2 Is there any limit to what the programme designers will think of?

3 Do you think reality TV shows like this one are OK?

4 Do you think the contestants in this programme will suffer bad effects?

5 Do you think that programmes like this humiliate the contestants?

(b) In what order do you think the interviewer asks the questions?

(c) Work with a partner. Discuss the answers you think the psychologist will give to each of the questions.

(d) 🔊 Listen to the interview and check the order of the questions.

(e) 🔊 Listen again and make notes about her answers.

(f) Use your notes to correct these statements.

1 Dr Wright watches reality TV shows for personal interest.

2 Dr Wright thinks the contestants on *Shattered* were awful.

3 Going without sleep will have a long-term physical effect.

4 Everybody finds it easy to deal with fame and money.

5 Dr Wright hopes to see a reality TV show about hunger.

6 Grammar

Modal verbs of obligation, prohibition and permission

(a) Look at these examples from the interview with the psychologist in Exercise 5d.

1 *Shattered was the programme in which people* **had to** *stay awake as long as possible.*

2 *People* **don't have to** *become contestants on these programmes.*

3 *If they want to, they* **can** *leave.*

4 *What* **can** *we expect next? A hunger programme where people* **mustn't** *eat for a week?*

Which sentence says:

a someone is allowed to do something?

b it is very important not to do something?

c it is not necessary for someone to do something?

d it was necessary for someone to do something?

(b) Match the sentences and pictures. Write 1–6 in the boxes.

1 'You can come in now.'

2 'We can't park here.'

3 'We have to wear a uniform.'

4 'You don't have to shout.'

5 'You mustn't talk in here.'

6 'You must be over 18 to go in.'

c Complete the sentences with a modal verb.

1 Hurry up – we _mustn't_ be late!
2 Sorry, sir – you _____ switch your mobile phone off on the plane.
3 Your computer's broken? Don't worry – you _____ use mine.
4 It's Anna's birthday on Friday – I _____ remember to buy a present for her.
5 It's only 8 o'clock, and school doesn't start until 9 – you _____ hurry!
6 Sorry, Alex – this is an exam, so you _____ use your dictionary.

7 Vocabulary

Extreme adjectives and modifiers

a Look at these sentences from the interview in Exercise 5d. What do *enormous*, *fantastic* and *starving* mean?

*But don't these programmes put people under **enormous** pressure?*

*I think the contestants were **fantastic**.*

*People mustn't eat for a week, until they're **starving**!*

b Match the adjectives 1–7 with the extreme adjectives a–g.

1 big   a fantastic
2 small   b enormous
3 tired   c boiling
4 hot   d exhausted
5 cold   e tiny
6 good   f starving
7 hungry   g freezing

c Here are some things that people said in the interview.

*That's not **very** difficult to deal with.*

*It's hard to deal with being **really** famous.*

*They'll be **absolutely** fine.*

Here are more examples of adjectives with the modifiers *very*, *really* and *absolutely*. Some you can use together and some you can't. Write a tick (✓) or a cross (✗) beside each one.

really small	✓	very small	✓	absolutely small	✗
really tiny		very tiny		absolutely tiny	
really hot		very hot		absolutely hot	
really boiling		very boiling		absolutely boiling	

d Complete the sentences with one of the adjectives in Exercise 7b. There may be more than one answer.

1 I burned my hand really badly. The water was absolutely _____ .
2 Let's go and get some food – I'm very _____ .
3 We stayed up all night to finish our work. The next day we were absolutely _____ .
4 When John got fired, the company only gave him a very _____ amount of money.
5 It's really _____ in here. Can I close the window?
6 She told us an absolutely _____ story.

e Work with a partner. Talk about the topics in the box. Express your opinions about them using extreme adjectives and modifiers.

a film you've seen
a holiday you've been on
a book you've read
a story you've heard

8 Listen and speak

a 🔊 Look at the picture and the title of the song. What do you think it is about? How do you think the man feels? Listen to the song (with your book closed) and check your ideas.

b 🔊 Listen to the song again. Eight words or phrases are wrong. Write the correct words.

Somebody's Watching Me
by Rockwell

I'm just an average man with an average life
I work from nine to five, hey hell, I pay the money
All I want is to be left alone in my average school
But why do I always feel like I'm in the Twilight Zone?

I always feel like somebody's watching me
And I have no privacy
I always feel like somebody's watching me
Tell me, is it just a dream?

When I go out at night
I bolt the door real tight
People call me on the phone I'm trying to invite
Well, can the people on the radio see me or am I just
     paranoid?

When I'm on the street, I'm afraid to wash my hair
'Cos I might open my eyes and find someone standing
     there
People say I'm healthy, just a little touched
But maybe showers remind me of Psycho
     too much
That's why ...

I always feel like somebody's watching me
And I have no privacy
I always feel like somebody's watching me
Who's playing tricks on me?

I don't know anymore
Are the teachers watching me?
Well, is the mailman watching me?
And I don't feel safe anymore, oh, what
     a mess
I wonder who's watching me now?
Who? The IRS?

I always feel like somebody's watching me
And I have no privacy
I always feel like somebody's watching me
Tell me, is it just a dream?

c Why do you think the singer feels so paranoid? In pairs, see who can make up the strangest story about what happened to him.

Did you know ...?

Rockwell is Kennedy Gordy, son of Tamla Motown Records founder Berry Gordy. Prince and Madonna were doing well with just one name – so Motown producers gave Kennedy the name Rockwell, after the American painter Norman Rockwell.

9 Vocabulary

Collocations with *on*

In the song in Exercise 10 the singer says '*Who's playing tricks on me?*'

Here are some other collocations with *on*. Complete the sentences with the words in the box.

| TV   time   the phone   strike   holiday   offer |

1   What's on _____ tonight? Another soap opera, I suppose?
2   I hear the factory's on _____ . They want more money.
3   You're always late! Why can't you arrive on _____ ?
4   I prefer text messaging to talking on _____ .
5   These trainers were on _____ at the sports shop. I got them for a really good price.
6   I can't wait until we're on _____ . I really need a rest!

10 Write

a Read the magazine article and answer the questions.

1   Who will the contestants be in the programme?
2   Where are they going to live?
3   What will each contestant be able to take with them?
4   How often will TV show scenes from the show?
5   How will the person who has to leave be chosen?
6   What are the prizes for the winner?

Cave People
coming our way

A new reality TV show called *Cave People* will be on our screens next year. Twelve celebrities (their names won't be revealed before the programme actually starts) will be taken to a place somewhere in the mountains of Wales.

They will live in a cave, with no modern equipment or food at all, although each star will be allowed to take one personal item. The stars will be filmed 24 hours a day – hunting for animals in the nearby forests, looking for wood and learning to make fire. Six times a day, there'll be clips on TV showing the most interesting scenes. Viewers at home will vote each week for the person who has to leave.

The star who survives all this will pick up £1,000,000 for charity – and a recording contract for a CD.

b Write a magazine article about a new reality TV show.
Use the questions to help you. Write 120–150 words.

Module 2 Check your progress

1 Grammar

a) Complete the sentences. Use the correct future form of the verb. The word at the end is to help you.

1 Sorry, I can't come tomorrow – I *'m seeing* (see) the doctor in the morning. *arrangement*

2 What _____ you _____ (wear) to the party tomorrow? *intention*

3 I _____ (not do) anything this evening. *arrangement*

4 Go and ask Amy – I'm sure she _____ (know) the answer. *prediction*

5 Our teacher _____ (take) us on a museum visit next week. *arrangement* [4]

b) Complete the sentences. Use the correct form of the first conditional.

1 It *won't work* (not work) unless you *switch* (switch) it on!

2 I _____ (call) you as soon as I _____ (get) home.

3 If you _____ (not come) inside now, you _____ (miss) the programme.

4 They _____ (not let) you in if you _____ (not be) over 18.

5 I _____ (see) you tonight, unless my brother _____ (ask) me to help with his homework. [4]

c) Rewrite the sentences, using the correct form of causative *have*.

1 Someone repaired my bike for me last week. I *had my bike repaired last week.*

2 Someone cuts Mr Hart's hair every month. Mr Hart _____ .

3 Someone has repaired our teacher's car. Our teacher _____ .

4 Someone is making a cake for Sally's birthday. Sally _____ .

5 Someone is going to install a new phone for us tomorrow. We're _____ . [4]

d) Complete the sentences. Use the correct form of the past simple passive or the present perfect passive.

1 The radio *was invented* (invent) at the beginning of the 20th century.

2 In the First World War, radios _____ (use) to communicate with soldiers.

3 Since the 1960s, many radio signals _____ (send) into outer space.

4 So far, no answers _____ (receive) from other planets.

5 It's possible that the signals have arrived on other planets, but the messages _____ (not understand). [4]

e) Complete the sentences. Use the correct form of the future passive.

> send   examine   not answer   ~~explore~~
> bring   find

1 The planet Mars *will be explored* during the next few years.

2 Special robot vehicles _____ to investigate the planet's surface.

3 Perhaps some evidence of life _____ there.

4 It's possible that rocks and dust from Mars _____ back to Earth.

5 These rocks _____ to find out if it is possible to live on Mars.

6 The questions about Mars _____ for a very long time. [5]

f) Complete the sentences. Use with the correct form of *make, let,* or *be allowed to*.

1 In football, only the goalkeeper *is allowed to* catch the ball.

2 My father never _____ me go into his office while he's working.

3 My friend lends me things – but he always _____ me promise to give them back!

4 _____ your school _____ you take mobile phones into classrooms?

5 We _____ (not) talk in examinations.

6 _____ your parents _____ you do housework? [5]

g) Complete the sentences. Use modal verbs of permission, obligation and prohibition.

1 My teacher caught me sleeping in class and I *had to* stay behind after class.

2 It's a really big secret, OK? You _____ tell anyone.

3 I _____ come to your party. Mum says I'm not allowed to.

4 _____ you _____ wear a uniform to school?

5 I'm not completely stupid, you know – you _____ explain *everything* to me! [4]

2 Vocabulary

a Complete the sentences with the words in the box.

> timetable   platform   ~~cruise~~   flight
> arrive at   boarding card   tour   arrive in

1. Last summer, we went on a two week _cruise_ around the Caribbean Islands.
2. You need to show your _____ to get on the plane.
3. This is my first time on a plane. I hope I'm not sick during the _____ !
4. Look at the _____ and see when the train arrives.
5. If we _____ the airport late, we'll miss the flight.
6. When we went to Paris, the first thing we did was go on a _____ of the city.
7. What time do we _____ London?
8. Oh no, I've left my bag on the _____ !

[ ] 7

b Write the correct form of *make* or *do* in each space.

1. You can work in my office – but please don't _make_ a mess, OK?
2. You failed the exam? Well, don't worry – I'm sure you _____ your best.
3. Yesterday I _____ a big effort and got up early!
4. I took some medicine for my cold, and it _____ me a lot of good. I'm fine now!
5. My uncle really enjoys _____ money!
6. Smile at people! It _____ a big difference, you know!
7. I'm working hard and I think I'm _____ a lot of progress.

[ ] 6

c Write the correct word in each space.

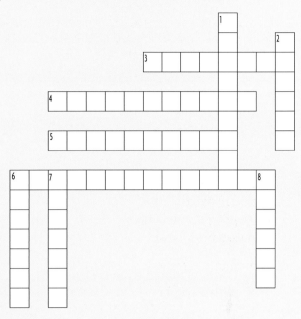

Across

3. A group of people who watch a film or play.
4. People who are famous (especially in the entertainment business).
5. Someone who competes on a quiz show.
6. It's a very popular programme – the _____ _____ are very high. (2 words)

Down

1. Someone who introduces a television or radio show.
2. A group of TV programmes about the same subject.
6. People who watch television.
7. A story on television is often divided into one _____ each week.
8. A funny TV programme with the same characters but a different story each programme.

[ ] 9

How did you do?

Tick (✓) a box for each section.

Total score:	☺	☹	☹
[ ] 52	Very good	OK	Not very good
Grammar	24 – 30	15 – 23	less than 15
Vocabulary	17 – 22	11 – 16	less than 11

Module 3
Right and wrong

YOU WILL LEARN ABOUT ...

- Some classic 'monsters' from fiction ....
- A computer game ....
- Graffiti ....
- Teenage crime ....
- The filming of *The Beach* ....
- The 1969 moon landing ....
- Mysterious places ....

 Can you match each picture with a topic?

YOU WILL LEARN HOW TO ...

Speak
- Talk about computer games
- Guess about your partner's habits
- Discuss graffiti
- Talk about getting into trouble
- Describe hypothetical situations
- Discuss crime and punishment
- Describe something you wish could be different
- Discuss the making of the film *The Beach*
- Talk about conspiracy theories
- Speculate about mysterious places

Write
- A discursive composition: presenting advantages and disadvantages
- A formal letter of opinion about crime
- A discursive composition: presenting arguments and giving your opinion
- A narrative: developing a story

Read
- Short introductions to classic novels
- An article about graffiti
- A questionnaire about honesty
- An article about the making of the film *The Beach*
- An extract from a story about hypnotism
- An article about two mysterious places

Listen
- A conversation about a computer game
- A dialogue about doing something wrong
- Interviews about teenage crime
- A radio programme about the first moon landing
- A radio interview about Seahenge
- A song

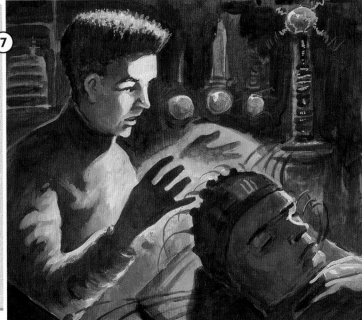

Use grammar

Can you match the names of the grammar points with the examples?

Verbs + gerunds and infinitives

Second conditional

I wish / if only + past simple

Linkers of contrast

Modals of deduction in the present

Indirect questions

Modals of deduction in the past

The murderer **must have been** a man.

I **remembered to post** the letter.

Do you know where she lives?

If I **knew** where she lived, I **would tell** you.

Although it was difficult, we all passed the test.

They **might be** Spanish.

I **wish I had** a car.

Use vocabulary

Can you think of two more examples for each topic?

Noun suffixes	Phrasal verbs with *down*	Crime	Problems
popular**ity**	break down	pay a fine	talk it over
relax**ation**	slow down	break the law	sleep on it
....	....	....	....
....	....	....	....

9 Good and evil

* Verbs + gerunds/infinitives review
* Verbs that take either gerund or infinitive
* Vocabulary: noun suffixes; belonging to a group

1 Read and listen

(a) Read the texts quickly and match them with the pictures.

1 THE PICTURE OF DORIAN GRAY
by Oscar Wilde

Dorian Gray is young and handsome and detests getting older. When he sees the portrait his friend Basil Hallward has painted of him he is filled with sadness. 'I want to be young forever, and this picture to grow old,' he says. 'I would give my soul for that.' Sometime later Dorian treats his girlfriend Sibyl Vane very badly and he notices that his face in the painting has changed – it is older and more cruel – but he is still young and beautiful. Is his wish starting to come true? Dorian decides to find out.

2 THE STRANGE CASE OF DOCTOR JEKYLL AND MR HYDE
by Robert Louis Stevenson

Doctor Jekyll believes that the human soul is part good, part evil. To prove his theory he invents a drink that turns him into the evil Mr. Hyde, a thief and a murderer, and back again. Dr Jekyll enjoys having another personality that he can control – until one day he goes to sleep as Jekyll and wakes up as Hyde. Hyde is starting to take control and Jekyll realises he must do something to stop him – but what?

3 FAUST
by Johann Wolfgang von Goethe

Dr Faust, a philosopher, is depressed. His search for the meaning of life is going nowhere. He is thinking about killing himself when the Devil appears in front of him, and suggests making a deal: Faust will get what he wants on Earth, if he promises to give the Devil his soul in return. Faust agrees and for the first time in his life he feels happy. Then a young girl called Margarete enters his life …

4 FRANKENSTEIN
by Mary Shelley

Victor Frankenstein is a scientist who imagines living in a world where people have the power over life and death. He wants to 'play God' and decides to build a human being from bits of dead bodies. As a bolt of lightning brings his creation to life, Frankenstein discovers he has made a monster. The monster disappears but two years later it returns and Frankenstein begins to realise the mistake he has made.

(b) 🔊 Read the texts again and listen. Answer the questions.

1 Who: a becomes two people?
   b doesn't want to get older?
   c makes a deal with the Devil?
   d wants control over life?
2 How has Dorian's face in the painting changed?
3 How does Dr Jekyll become Mr Hyde?
4 What is Faust's deal with the Devil?
5 What does Frankenstein use to build a human being?

2 Grammar

Verbs + gerunds

(a) Look at the sentences. The missing verbs are followed by a verb in the *-ing* form (a gerund). Use the texts in Exercise 1a to complete the sentences.

1   Dorian Gray .... getting older.
2   Dr Jekyll .... having another personality.
3   The Devil .... making a deal with Faust.
4   Frankenstein .... living in a different world.

(b) The verbs *enjoy, detest, don't mind, imagine, feel like, suggest, practise, miss* and *can't stand* are all followed by a gerund.

(c) Complete the story extract with the verbs in the box.

| ~~move~~ | cross | go | hear | sing | see | have | shout |

A few years ago, we lived in a house by the sea but then my parents suggested [1] *...moving...* to another house, in the town centre. So we moved.

It was OK living in the city – I enjoyed [2] .... to the shopping centre near my new home, for example, and I didn't mind [3] .... other houses from my window – but I detested [4] .... all those busy streets! Sometimes I felt like [5] .... at the drivers of all those cars!

I always loved living by the sea, and I missed [6] .... the sound of the waves outside our old house. Sometimes I imagined [7] .... a house of my own, on the beach, where I could live alone and practise [8] .... without annoying anyone! I also missed Jacob, but that wasn't a problem with living in the town. Jacob was dead.

Verbs + infinitives

(d) Underline the verbs in these sentences.

1   Dorian wants to stay young forever.
2   Faust promises to give the Devil his soul.
3   Frankenstein decides to build a human being.

(e) The verbs *hope, promise, ask, learn, expect, decide, afford, offer, choose* and *want* are followed by a verb in the infinitive form.

(f) Complete the sentences with a verb from box A and a verb from box B. Make any necessary changes to the verbs.

A hope   learn   not expect
decide   ~~promise~~   offer

B do   live   help   play
~~buy~~   go

1   My parents have *promised to buy* me a bike for my birthday.
2   The cinema was full last night, so we .... to a café instead.
3   When I'm older, I .... in New York or San Francisco.
4   My brother .... me with my Maths homework.
5   My sister .... tennis – and she's making good progress!
6   I'm just amazed at my exam results – I .... so well!

3 Speak

(a) Work with a partner. How well do you know them? Take a guess and complete the sentences for them.

- For your next birthday, you hope ...
- At the weekend, you really enjoy ...
- For your next holiday, you want ...

(b) Compare your ideas with your partner.

4 Speak and listen

(a) Work with a partner and answer these questions.

1 Look at the woman in the picture. What do you know about her?

2 Do you often play computer games? (Why / Why not?)

(b) 🔊 Listen to Charlotte talking to Jessica about a Lara Croft computer game. Circle the name of the game.

1 *Into the Darkness*
2 *The Monster of Loch Ness*
3 *Another Day in Darkness*
4 *The Angel of Darkness*

(c) 🔊 Listen again and circle the correct answers.

1 Charlotte thinks the game is different because Lara:
   a works for the army
   b is hunted
   c kills a good person
   d falls ill

2 After a phone call from a friend called Werner von Croy, Lara:
   a goes to Paris
   b goes to Prague
   c goes to London
   d goes to Amsterdam

3 Lara is hunted by the police because they think:
   a she's murdered her friend
   b she's stolen an old painting
   c she's escaped from the police
   d she's the Queen of the Darkness

4 Lara escapes and follows Eckhardt. Later he:
   a asks her to marry him
   b wants to become president
   c decides to buy a hotel
   d threatens to attack the world

5 Vocabulary

Noun suffixes

(a) Which of the underlined words is a noun? Which is a verb?

1 I really can't <u>imagine</u> a more interesting computer game.

2 It doesn't take much <u>imagination</u> to figure out who wins in the end.

(b) Look at these common ways of making nouns from verbs and adjectives:

–ation	–ion	–ness
imagine → imagination	protect → protection	kind → kindness
–ment	**–ence**	**–ity**
enjoy → enjoyment	different → difference	possible → possibility

(c) Work in pairs. How many other examples can you think of? Add them to the examples in Exercise 6b. Use them to test another pair.

(d) Make nouns from the verbs and adjectives. Use the nouns to complete the sentences below.

agree   prefer   react   entertain   prepare
popular   ~~relax~~

1 Listening to music, for me, is the best kind of _relaxation_ that there is.

2 Madonna is still a very successful singer. Her _____ is enormous.

3 If you haven't got much time, make a fruit salad. It doesn't need a lot of _____ .

4 My father wanted to buy that car, but he couldn't come to an _____ with the owner.

5 I was surprised by her _____ when I told her about the plan.

6 What did people do for _____ before TV?

7 Either tea or coffee is fine – I don't have a _____ .

6 Pronunciation

Stress in nouns, adjectives and verbs

🔊 Turn to page 120.

7 Grammar

Verbs with gerunds or infinitives

a The verbs *like, love, hate, prefer, begin* and *start* are usually followed by a gerund, but an infinitive can also be used. There is no difference in meaning.

I started reading when I was four.
I started to read when I was four.

Remember and *stop* can be followed by either a gerund or the infinitive – but the meaning is different.

I remember talking to my sister about it. (= I talked to her in the past and <u>now</u> I remember that.)

If I remember to talk to my sister, then you can have the game. (= Perhaps I will remember and <u>then</u> I will talk to her.)

I stopped eating chocolate six months ago. (= I ate chocolate until six months ago but <u>then</u> I stopped.)

I was in town shopping, and I stopped to eat a sandwich. (= I stopped and <u>then</u> I ate a sandwich.)

b (Circle) the correct form of the verb in each sentence.

1 I remember *to meet / meeting* Ken in Paris. I think it was three or four years ago.

2 Don't worry – I'll remember *to give / giving* you the book back.

3 Please stop *to make / making* such a noise! I want to go to sleep!

4 It was really hot in the car, so we stopped *to buy / buying* some ice creams.

c Fill in the correct form of the verbs.

1 How did you forget there was a test today? I remember .... (tell) you about it.

2 He's a nice guy, but he never stops .... (talk) about football!

3 I need to talk to Lucy – I must remember .... (phone) her when I get home.

4 I saw Rob in town yesterday, so I stopped .... (say) hello.

5 I know I locked the door. I remember .... (lock) it.

6 I'm really hungry. Can we stop .... (get) a sandwich?

7 Please remember .... (post) my letter.

8 Suddenly everybody stopped .... (shout). There was silence.

Look

would like / would love / would hate / would prefer are always followed by the infinitive.

I would like to go to the cinema.

8 Speak

a Work with a partner. Student B: Turn to page 122. Student A: Write your answers to these things on a piece of paper.

● Something you must remember to do next week.

● Something you like doing when you find it difficult to relax.

● Something you started doing when you were a teenager.

● Something you hate doing.

b Look at your partner's answers and guess what they refer to. You start.

walking to school

A: *Is that something you hate doing?*

B: *No, that's something I stopped doing when I became a teenager. I stopped walking and started cycling to school.*

Culture in mind

9 Read

a Read the article and match the titles with the paragraphs. Write A–E in the boxes. There is one title you do not need to use.

A Bringing people together   D Street art and hip-hop culture

B Lessons on the streets   E How to speak graffiti

C But is it music?

b Mark the statements *T* (true) or *F* (false). Correct the false statements.

1 TAKI 183 was a teenage graffiti artist. ☐

2 The graffiti scheme in Rochdale is for teenagers only. ☐

3 People did not like using the subway before the graffiti artists came. ☐

4 Since the scheme started, more people have started to vandalise walls in the town. ☐

5 Temper's Art teacher didn't think he was very good. ☐

6 Most of the other graffiti artists were about ten years older than Temper. ☐

7 Temper is involved in many different sides of hip-hop culture. ☐

8 *Crews*, *writers* and *burners* are all people. ☐

THE WRITING'S ON THE WALL

1 ☐ Is it art or is it just vandalism? Well, it's still a crime, but graffiti has changed since the days of spraying your name on a wall to mark your territory. Street art has become much more sophisticated since a 17-year-old called Demetrius started spraying his 'tag', TAKI 183, all over the New York underground in 1971, and hip-hop culture was born. Hip-hop is a mixture of art, music and dancing, poetry, language and fashion. It came from young inner-city people, who felt left out by their richer classmates and who were desperate to express themselves in any way they could.

2 ☐ An experiment to control the spread of graffiti in Rochdale, Greater Manchester, has been so successful that plans have been made by local street artists for an international convention in June. 'We're planning to get people together from different countries like France and Germany for a week,' says Liam, one of the organisers. The scheme started in 2000, and has attracted people of all age groups and both sexes. 'We all share a common interest and get on really well with each other.' The first site to be chosen was a subway. 'Before we began, people were afraid to use the subway. We had it cleaned up and now, with all the artists hanging out down there, people are using it again. People can relate to graffiti much more now.' By providing places to display their talents legally, there has been a fall in the amount of 'tagging' on people's private property.

3 ☐ Street artist Temper developed his drawing skills at a young age. In art classes at school he was really frustrated because the Art teacher didn't spend time with him. They thought he was already very good at Art and so spent more time with other students. So, at 12 years old, Temper started painting with all these guys he'd hooked up with who were about 22 years old. He looked up to them and loved what they were doing on the streets of Wolverhampton, England. 'The whole hip-hop scene was built up of different things and I did a bit of everything: beat-boxing, body popping and DJ-ing. But it was always the graffiti I was best at,' he says.

10 Vocabulary

Belonging to a group

a Replace the underlined words with one of the phrases in the box. Check your answers in the text.

> relate to   hook up with
> look up to   hang out (with)
> feel left out (by)

1   ... with all the artists <u>spending time together</u> down there, people are using it again.
2   He <u>admired</u> them and loved what they were doing.
3   ... painting walls with all these guys he'd <u>made friends with</u>.
4   ... young inner-city people who <u>weren't accepted by</u> their richer classmates.
5   People can <u>understand</u> graffiti much more now.

4 ☐ **A WRITER**
a graffiti artist

A CREW
organised group of writers

A TAG
a writer's name or signature

A THROW UP
a more developed tag, with two colours or more

A PIECE
a writer's painting, short for *masterpiece*; must have at least three colours

A BURNER
a technical, stylish piece, generally done in bright colours

STYLE WARS
competition between artists to choose the most creative piece

Discussion box

Work in pairs or small groups. Discuss these questions together.

1   Is there any graffiti in your home town?
2   What kind of people do you think do this, and why?

b Work in small groups. Ask and answer questions about families, friends and groups using the vocabulary.

> What kind of people do you usually like to hang out with?

> Who do you look up to most in your family?

11 Write

a Read the composition and answer the questions.

1   Which paragraph talks about the advantages of graffiti walls? What are they?
2   Which paragraph talks about the disadvantages of graffiti walls? What are they?
3   Does the writer think graffiti walls are a good or bad thing?

What are the advantages and disadvantages of organised graffiti walls in city centres?

Graffiti is a serious problem and the fact it is a crime doesn't stop young people leaving their 'mark' on public and private buildings. <u>Because of</u> graffiti, many of our city centres and housing estates seem dirty and dangerous. To stop this 'social disease', many town councils have organised 'graffiti walls' – special places where graffiti artists can practise their art legally.

Graffiti walls bring teenagers together and help them to be creative. <u>In addition</u>, they show street artists how to use their art in a good way. But the greatest advantage is that they help stop graffiti on buildings. Statistics show that cities with graffiti walls have less vandalism.

<u>On the other hand</u>, there are people who think that graffiti walls do nothing to solve the problem. In fact they argue that graffiti walls can make the problem worse, because they make the crime seem OK.

<u>To sum up</u>, there are both advantages and disadvantages to organised graffiti walls. I believe that the advantages are much greater. I think they are an excellent way to help with the problem of the graffiti in many of our cities.

b Which of the underlined words in the text are used to introduce:

1   the conclusion?
2   another point supporting the previous ideas?
3   the opposite side of an argument?
4   the consequence of an action?

c Write your own composition about one of the following topics. Use the composition on graffiti to help you. Remember to use topic sentences. Write 120–180 words.

● What are the advantages and disadvantages of the Internet?
● What are the good and bad sides of playing computer games?

For your portfolio

⑩ Getting into trouble

* Second conditional review
* *I wish / if only* for present situations
* Vocabulary: crime
* Vocabulary: phrasal verbs with *down*

Story 1

1 Speak and listen

a Work with a partner. Look at the pictures and discuss how you think these stories end.

b 🔊 Listen to Megan and Steve telling the two stories. Check your ideas in Exercise 1a. Did Steve and Megan get caught, or did they get away with what they did?

c Work with a partner. Discuss the questions.

  1 Which of the things they did was worse, in your opinion? Why?

  2 Think about when you were at junior school. Can you remember something you did that got you into trouble? Tell your partner about it.

Story 2

2 Read

Work with a partner. Ask the questions in the questionnaire and tick (✓) your partner's answers. Use the 'Score for answers' to find your total. Then turn to page 128 and tell your partner the result.

ARE YOU *REALLY* HONEST? Try our questionnaire – *and tell the truth!*

1 If you bought something, and the shop assistant gave you too much change by mistake, would you:
  a pick up the money and leave the shop with a smile?
  b tell the shop assistant that they had made a mistake?
  c take it and put it in a charity box?

2 Imagine you received an email by mistake that was really for a friend of yours. Would you:
  a read it and delete it – you thought it wasn't important?
  b read it and then send it to the right person?
  c not read it, and immediately send it back to the writer?

3 Suppose you were doing an examination, and there was a question you weren't sure about but you could see what the person next to you was writing. Would you:
  a look a little bit, just to help you think more clearly?
  b copy their answer, but change it a little?
  c not look, and do your best to answer it yourself?

4 Say a friend lent you a CD, and you really liked it. When your friend asked for it back, would you:
  a say 'What CD?'
  b get it, and give it back immediately?
  c tell them you hadn't listened to it yet, and ask to keep it longer?

5 If you had a really important party to go to but couldn't afford anything new to wear. Would you:
  a buy something from a shop and take it back after the party?
  b ask your brother or sister to lend you something?
  c take something from your brother's or sister's room?

Scores for answers:
1 a: 0 b: 4 c: 2 2 a: 0 b: 2 c: 4
3 a: 0 b: 0 c: 4 4 a: 0 b: 4 c: 2
5 a: 0 b: 4 c: 2

3 Grammar

Second conditional review

a Look at the example. Is this about something that really happened or is it only imaginary?

*If a shop assistant **gave** you too much change by mistake, **would you take** it?*

b Complete the rule with *could*, *past*, *might* and *would*.

> **Rule:**
> - We use *if* with the _____ tense (to introduce the condition), and _____ + the infinitive (to show the consequence) when we want to show that a situation is unreal or unlikely.
> - It is also possible to use _____ (for possibility and ability) or _____ (for uncertainty) in place of *would* (for certainty).

> **Look**
> Notice the use of the comma:
> *If you failed your exams, would you leave school?*
> *Would you leave school if you failed your exams?*

c Complete the sentences. Use the correct form of the second conditional.

1 If you _____ (find) a watch in the street, what would you do with it?
2 I _____ (send) her a postcard if I knew her address.
3 If I had more money, I _____ (go out) more.
4 If you _____ (not go) to bed late every night, you wouldn't be so tired.
5 What _____ you _____ if you won £1 million?
6 I wouldn't need a car if I _____ (live) in the city.
7 If you told me a secret, I _____ (not tell) anyone.
8 If I _____ (go) to Brazil, I could learn Portuguese.

First conditional vs. second conditional

d Which is first conditional, which is second conditional? Which situation is more likely to happen?

*If my dad **gave** me a new car, I'd **be** really happy.*
*If my dad **gives** me a new car, I'll **be** really happy.*

e Match, and complete the sentences.

1 If I get married next year,
  If I got married next year,
    a I wouldn't *go to university.*
    b my parents will *be very surprised.*

2 If I go out this weekend,
  If I went out this weekend,
    a I'll …
    b I'd …

3 If I get a good job when I leave school,
  If I got a good job when I left school,
    a I would …
    b I'll …

f Find other ways in the questionnaire to introduce imaginary situations.

_____ *if* _____   _____   _____   _____

4 Speak

Complete the questions, add two more questions, then ask a partner.

1 If you could go anywhere in the world, where …?
2 Suppose you could meet anyone in the world. Who …?
3 Imagine you met your sporting hero. What …?
4 Say you could change one thing about yourself. What …?

5 Listening and vocabulary
Crime

(a) 🔊 Match the words with the pictures. Write 1–6 in the boxes. Then listen, check and repeat.

1 burglary	2 joyriding	3 arson
4 shoplifting	5 pick-pocketing	
6 vandalism		

(a)

(b)

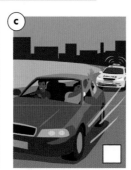
(c)

(d)

(e)

(f)

(b) 🔊 Listen to the radio show and tick (✓) the crimes that are mentioned.

(c) 🔊 Listen again and use the words in the box to complete the table.

burglary   excitement   joyriding   fun
shoplifting   vandalism   money

	Crime	Reason
Chloe	....	....fun....
Ian	....	....
	....	
Liam	....	....

(d) 🔊 Work with a partner and answer these questions. Then listen again and check.

1 Where did Chloe spray paint her name?
2 How does Chloe feel now?
3 Why did Ian stop doing burglary?
4 How does Ian get money now?
5 When did Liam usually go joyriding?
6 What did the police do?

6 Speaking and vocabulary
Crime

(a) Use the correct form of the verbs in the box to complete the text.

break   do (x2)   commit   pay   get (x3)
send   put

Most teenagers [1]........... into trouble sometime in their life. But there's a big difference between [2]........... something wrong like staying out too late, and [3]........... a crime. The rise in teenage crime is a serious problem for our society. When a young person [4]........... the law and [5]........... away with it, they are likely to repeat the crime. Therefore, when a teenager [6]........... caught we must do everything to show them that this is not true. [7]........... them to prison is not the answer – they will only meet more experienced criminals there. Most of them don't have the money to [8]........... a fine, so one good option is to [9]........... them on probation. This means they have a period of time when they must not commit any more crimes. If they do, they will be sent to prison. But the best punishment is getting them to [10]........... community service – for example, cleaning rubbish off the streets or gardening in public parks. This is the best way of teaching them that they have a responsibility to the society they are part of.

(b) Look at the text again. The writer mentions four types of punishment. What are they?

(c) Work with a partner and discuss these questions.

1 Who do you usually get in trouble with most and why?
2 What crimes do young people in your country commit?
3 What small things do people do every day that are actually breaking the law, for example, dropping litter?
4 What punishments do you think are best for young offenders?

7 Grammar

I wish / if only

(a) Look at these examples from the interviews in Exercise 6b.

I wish there was more to do in this town.
If only I had more money.

1 In the first sentence, does the speaker think there is enough to do in the town? How do they feel about this?

2 In the second sentence, does the speaker think they have enough money? How do they feel about this?

3 What tense is used after *I wish* and *if only*?

(b) Use the verbs in the box in the correct tense to complete the sentences.

be	be	not have
know	play	understand

8 Speak

(a) Work with a partner. Look at the painting and think of five thoughts the characters might have. Start with *I wish ...* or *If only ...*

If only I could have a rest!

(b) Work with a partner and look at the topics in the box. What would you like to be different about each of these things?

the town you live in	your home life	possessions
abilities	interests	school/college	the world

Do you wish there were more cafés in this town?
Do you ever think 'If only there was more to do at the weekends'?

9 Pronunciation

I wish ... and *if only ...*

🔊 Turn to page 121.

1 If only I .... maths.

2 If only I .... as intelligent as Tom Jacobs.

3 I wish I .... so much homework tonight.

4 If only I .... how to talk to girls.

5 I wish I .... as good-looking as Ryan Brown.

6 I wish I .... football as well as Ryan Brown.

A problem for Matt

10 Read and listen

(a) 🔊 What is Matt's problem? What is he going to do about it? Read, listen and check your answers.

Ben: Great party, eh, Caroline?

Caroline: Yeah!

Matt: Hey, you two. Enjoying yourselves?

Caroline: Yes thanks, Matt. But what about you? You look like you've got something on your mind.

Matt: Yeah, sort of. But it's my problem, not yours.

Ben: Oh, Matt. We're friends, right? We'd like to help if we can.

Caroline: That's right. Come on, Matt – Joanne told me you're in some kind of trouble, so what is it?

Matt: OK. I owe someone quite a lot of money, and it's getting me down.

Caroline: We can see that, Matt. Tell us about it.

Matt: Well, I've been really stupid, that's all. You see, about four weeks ago, I bought a second-hand motorbike from this guy in my street, for £900. I gave him £500, and I promised him the rest this week ... and I haven't got it. And he's going to kill me!

Caroline: Oh, Matt, I'm sure it's not that bad. He's not really going to kill you, is he?

Matt: I wouldn't be so sure! You don't know this guy!

Ben: Well, the way I see it, you should just give him the bike and ask him for your money back.

Caroline: I think Ben's right.

Matt: Maybe I could ask the bank to lend me the money.

Caroline: No, Matt, if you did that, you'd still have the problem of paying the money back!

Ben: And besides, you'd have to pay interest, and that's really bad news!

Matt: Well, yeah, that's a good point. So, what do I do?

Caroline: Why don't you just go and talk to the guy? Perhaps he'll let you pay him next month.

Ben: Yeah – try that. You never know! I'll come with you if you like.

Matt: Maybe you're right. I'll talk to him. But you know the worst thing? The motorbike's broken down three times since I bought it!

(b) Match the two parts of the sentences.

1	Matt's problem	a	he'll have to pay back more money than he borrows.
2	Matt has bought	b	some more money to pay for the motorbike.
3	Matt only paid	c	a used motorbike.
4	Matt has to find	d	is about money.
5	If Matt gets money from a bank,	e	has stopped working several times.
6	Matt's also unhappy because the bike	f	part of the price of the motorbike.

11 Everyday English

a Find expressions 1–4 in the story. Who says them?

1 the way I see it   2 and besides
3 that's a good point   4 you never know

Which one is used:

a to agree with someone? ☐

b when you are not sure if something will happen, but want to be encouraging? ☐

c to introduce an opinion? ☐

d to introduce an extra idea to an argument or opinion? ☐

b Use one of the phrases to complete each space.

A: I need some help with my homework.

B: Sorry, I can't help you right now. I've got lots of work to do myself – [1]_____ , it's *your* problem, not mine!

A: We get too much homework!

B: Really? Well [2]_____ , we have to do homework to learn properly.

A: Well, yes, [3]_____ .

B: And we might not get homework next week – [4]_____ !

12 Vocabulary

Phrasal verbs with *down*

a Match the underlined verbs with the meanings.

1 It's getting me down.
2 She was offered a good job but she turned it down.
3 The motorbike's broken down three times.
4 We're going too fast – can you slow down?

a stop working
b to make someone unhappy, depressed
c not accept
d reduce the speed

b Complete each sentence with one of the phrasal verbs above, in the correct form.

1 Andy! Don't speak so quickly! _____ a little!
2 I was late home on Saturday because the bus _____ and we had to wait for another one.
3 Sarah hates getting bad marks – it always _____ her _____ .
4 I asked her if she wanted to go to the cinema but she _____ me _____ .

13 Write

a Read the newspaper report and the letter. What problem is Roger Davis writing about? What action does he suggest?

b Write a letter to the newspaper from the point of view of a teenager living in the town. Write 120–180 words.

YOUNG PEOPLE AND CRIME

Statistics show that more under-18-year-olds in our town have been convicted of shoplifting and burglary than ever. Small crimes like vandalism and graffiti have gone up by 20% compared to last year.

Dear Sir or Madam

I am writing to express my concern at the latest crime statistics reported in last Tuesday's *Evening Herald*.

The reason why we are seeing an increase in teenage crime is because this town offers very little for young people to do. Where is our sports centre, our cinema and our community projects? Teenagers need more than TV to keep them busy at night. If we don't offer them something, we cannot really be surprised when we wake up to find more graffiti on our walls and more of our houses burgled.

I suggest a town meeting where members of the public (including the young) can try and work out a solution to this problem before it gets any worse.

Yours faithfully

Roger Davis

Roger Davis

11 Two sides to every story

* Linkers of contrast
* Modal verbs of deduction (present)
* Vocabulary: problems

1 Read

(a) In 1998, a film crew went to Thailand to make a film of Alex Garland's book *The Beach*. The film's producer needed to find a paradise beach. What do you know about the film?

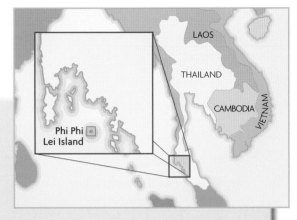

LAOS

THAILAND

CAMBODIA

VIETNAM

Phi Phi Lei Island

(b) Work with a partner. Student B: Turn to page 122. Student A: Read text A and answer the questions.

1 How did the film crew change the beach?

2 What was the result of planting coconut trees?

3 What did they do to make the sand stay on the beach? Did it work?

4 Did it rain more than normal?

5 Did the film crew pay a lot of money to the local people?

6 What did tourists think of the island when they visited it after the film was made?

(c) Work with your partner. Student A is a member of the film crew and Student B is an inhabitant of Phi Phi Lei. Discuss the questions in Exercise 1b. Are your answers the same?

Text A

One problem for our producer Andrew Macdonald was to find a place that looked like nobody had ever been there, and at the same time make it comfortable for a large film crew. We thought it over, and in the end, we made up our minds to use Phi Phi Lei Island, which had a wonderful deserted beach with a coral reef. Although the beach we found was incredible, it wasn't really flat enough to film on, so we sorted the problem out by using a bulldozer on it.

Tropical paradises usually have beaches with palm trees, but this beach didn't have a single one. We came up with the idea of planting some coconut palms to make it more beautiful. It worked really well. It looked even more beautiful. We put wooden poles on the beach to stop the sand from sliding into the sea, but there was some very heavy rain while we were there, more than normal, I think, and the beach didn't look so good for a while. We talked it over with the locals and paid $100,000 for damage, and I think that was very good money for them.

Despite these problems, it was a good experience for the islanders, because after people saw the film, lots of tourists came to Phi Phi Lei and thought it was paradise.

2 Grammar

Linkers of contrast: *however / although / even though / in spite of / despite*

(a) (Circle) the correct option. Find the sentences in the texts A and B in Exercise 1b to check your answers.

1 *Although / Despite* the beach we found was incredible, it wasn't really flat enough to film on.

2 *Despite / Although* these problems, it was a good experience for the islanders.

3 They put in some coconut trees to make it look 'more beautiful'. *Despite / However,* these trees are not native to our island.

4 *Even though / In spite* of this protection, the normal monsoon rain washed the sand into the sea.

5 *Even though / However,* they gave us money, it wasn't enough to really help us.

(b) Look at the sentences in Exercise 2a and complete the rule with *although, despite, in spite of, even though* and *however*.

Rule:

To introduce contrast:

● We use a subject + verb after _____ and

_____ .

_____ **he has** *a French mother, he doesn't speak any French.*

● We use a noun or verb in the *-ing form* after _____ and _____ .

_____ **having** *a French mother, he doesn't speak any French.*

_____ **his French mother,** *he doesn't speak any French.*

● We use _____ with a comma at the beginning of a sentence, or at the end.

His mother is French. _____ *, he doesn't speak any French.*

His mother is French. He doesn't speak any French, _____ *.*

(c) Combine the two ideas. Use the linker at the end. There may be more than one possible answer.

1 I'm going for a run. It's raining. (**despite**)
I'm going for a run, despite the rain.

2 I'm going for a run. It's raining. (**even though**)
----

3 The bus was late. We arrived on time. (**although**)
----

4 The garden isn't very nice. I like the house. (**however**)
----

5 They have lots of money. They aren't happy. (**in spite of**)
----

6 People have skin. Animals have fur. (**however**)
----

7 She went to see the film. She'd seen it before. (**despite**)
----

8 He passed the exam. He didn't study. (**even though**)
----

9 I didn't like the book. I enjoyed the film. (**although**)
----

10 She was cold. She didn't wear a jacket. (**in spite of**)
----

3 Pronunciation

/əʊ/ *though*

◁)) Turn to page 121.

Look

When using *in spite of* or *despite* in the negative, we use *not*.

Despite **not** *being invited, we still went to the party.* (Not: ~~Not despite being invited…~~)

In spite of **not** *having any of her own, she gets on really well with children.*

4 Listen

(a) How much do you know about the first moon landing? Answer these questions with a partner.

1 Who said 'That's one small step for man, one giant leap for mankind.'?
2 When was the first moon landing?
3 What nationality was the first man on the moon?

(b) 🔊 Listen to the start of the radio programme and check.

(c) Look at the words in the box. Find the items in the photos.

> moon buggy   reflection   shadow
> astronaut   light source   crater
> surface of the moon   sky

(d) 🔊 Listen to the next part of the programme. You will hear a professor talk about why he thinks the moon landing didn't really happen. Tick (✓) the words in the box that he uses to explain his theory.

(e) Work with a partner. Can you think of any arguments against Professor Hartson's ideas?

(f) 🔊 Listen to a NASA spokeswoman answer Professor Hartson's theories. Mark the statements *T* (true) or *F* (false). Correct the false statements.

1 Two light sources would result in one set of shadows. ☐
2 The surface of the moon is very flat. ☐
3 The surface of the moon reflects the sun. ☐
4 The stars are very near. ☐
5 It is possible to take a photo of a person with stars behind them. ☐

5 Speak

The professor's ideas on the moon landing are an example of a conspiracy theory. A conspiracy theory is when people don't believe the official story about a subject. They believe that something is being kept secret.

Work in groups of four. What other conspiracy theories do you know of? Discuss what you know about them and then present your ideas to the class.

6 Grammar

Modal verbs of deduction (present)

a Look at these examples and answer the questions.

*This **can't be** a photo of the moon because there are no stars.*
*Because of the shadows this photo **must be** a fake.*
*The astronaut **might be** in a studio.*
*I know people **could be** shocked to hear that the moon landing never happened.*

1 In which sentences is the speaker sure they are right?
2 In which sentences is the speaker not so sure?
3 What is the opposite of *must be*?

b Complete the sentences with *must be, can't be* or *might be*.

1 You've been walking all day. You _____ tired.
2 You think Maths is interesting! You _____ serious.
3 Be careful with that dog. I think it _____ dangerous.
4 It _____ that difficult. Even my little brother knows how to do it.
5 You really want to go bungee jumping? You _____ mad.
6 A: Do you know where Gemma is?
   B: She _____ in her room. I'm not sure.
7 You _____ hungry already, you've just had lunch.

c 🔊 Work with a partner. Look at the pictures and listen. Which picture do you hear? Discuss with your partner. Use *must be, can't be, could be* or *might be*. Write 1–3 in the boxes. There is one picture you do not need to use.

7 Vocabulary

Problems

a Read the text and match the underlined words with the definitions.

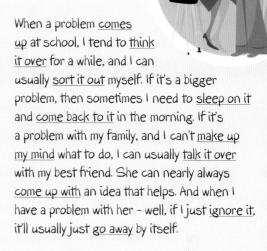

When a problem <u>comes up</u> at school, I tend to <u>think it over</u> for a while, and I can usually <u>sort it out</u> myself. If it's a bigger problem, then sometimes I need to <u>sleep on it</u> and <u>come back to it</u> in the morning. If it's a problem with my family, and I can't <u>make up my mind</u> what to do, I can usually <u>talk it over</u> with my best friend. She can nearly always <u>come up with</u> an idea that helps. And when I have a problem with her – well, if I just <u>ignore it</u>, it'll usually just <u>go away</u> by itself.

1 find a solution   ....
2 discuss it   ....
3 take more time   ....
4 think about it   ....
5 decide   ....
6 pretend it's not there ....
7 appear   ....
8 disappear   ....
9 find   ....
10 return   ....

b Complete the sentences with the words from the text in the correct form.

1 I don't like to *sleep on* a problem. I like to _____ everything _____ before I go to bed.
2 It seems that every day a new problem _____ in my life.
3 I hate decisions. I'm not very good at _____ .
4 My mother is the best person to _____ a problem with. She always _____ the best ideas.
5 The best way to solve a problem is to _____ it. Just let it _____ by itself.

c Tell your partner which of the sentences are true for you.

Fiction in mind

8 Read

(a) Have you ever seen a hypnotist's show? If you have, tell a partner what happened. If you haven't, what type of things do you think happen? Read the text and check your ideas.

The Real Aunt Molly

from: *The Fruitcake Special and other stories*
by Frank Brennan

The story

After her husband dies, Aunt Molly seems to lose all interest in life. Then one day her twin sons persuade her to go and watch a TV show being recorded in a studio and she is invited on stage to be hypnotised ...

Aunt Molly, for some reason, was an especially easy person to hypnotise. As she sat on a chair she 'went to sleep' to the sound of Maxwell's voice like a baby. We all wondered what hypnotic suggestions Maxwell would give her. Then Maxwell turned to Winston and said:

'What suggestions would you like to make, young man?' a _____1_____

The audience laughed.

The twins whispered to each other, then Winston spoke. 'Well ... Mum's always needed a bit more confidence, so what could you do to make her more ... '

'Decisive!' said Clement.

'That's it,' said Winston. 'More able to make decisions and be more confident – let her live life to the full!'

'Let's see what we can do,' said Maxwell. He first asked for her name and Grandpa told him. Then Maxwell turned to Aunt Molly who was still fast asleep. 'Now, Molly, you will answer only to my voice, do you understand?' b _____

'You will be a confident woman, full of strength. Whatever you want to do, you will succeed in doing. c _____ Is that clear to you, Molly?' said Maxwell.

Molly said that it was.

'When I tell you to open your eyes you will be that intelligent, confident woman; you will live life to the full. You will not remember that you have been hypnotised but you will be a new, confident woman who will live life to the full. You will continue until I – and only I – tell you to return to your normal life. Is that understood, Molly?' said Maxwell loudly and with quite a lot of confidence of his own.

Molly said she understood.

'Now, Molly,' said Maxwell. 'Open your eyes ...' But as he said this he suddenly gave a loud cry and fell at Aunt Molly's feet while holding on to his tie. His face had turned grey. Maxwell Marvel had a heart attack just as Aunt Molly was opening her eyes. d _____

She turned to the nearest person in the audience and said, 'Well, don't just sit there, man! This man has obviously had a heart attack – call for a doctor and an ambulance at once. He needs immediate attention.'

★ ★ ★

A man from the television company spoke to the audience and explained that, because of Maxwell Marvel's sudden and unfortunate accident, the show was at an end. e _____

Somebody behind us called out that it had been the best part of the show.

Grandpa went up to the man who had spoken to us. f _____

'You heard Maxwell,' the man told him. 'Only his voice can undo the orders. I'm sorry – you'll have to wait until Maxwell can speak to her himself.'

'But what if ...,' asked Grandpa, '... what if he doesn't get better?'

(b) Read the extract from the story again and add the sentences. Write 1–8 in the spaces. There are two sentences you do not need to use.

1 ~~'I'll tell this lovely lady to do anything that won't get her into trouble with the police!'~~

2 'Nothing is too difficult for you.'

3 'This ice cream is fantastic!'

4 'I understand,' said Molly quietly, though she was still asleep.

5 He said that he was very sorry that things had been cut short in this way.

6 The first thing she saw was Maxwell Marvel lying at her feet.

7 He said his tea was getting cold.

8 He asked him what they could do to get Aunt Molly back to normal now that Maxwell Marvel wasn't here.

(c) Answer these questions.

1 What was the relationship between Winston and the woman who was hypnotised?

2 What does the narrator tell us about the woman's usual personality?

3 Did the hypnotist do what he had promised to do? What evidence is there in the text?

4 Why did Grandpa talk to the man from the television company?

Discussion box

Work in pairs or small groups. Discuss these questions together.

1 Why do you think the story is called *The Real Aunt Molly*?

2 What might happen if the hypnotist can't undo his orders?

9 Write

(a) Read the composition quickly. How many negative points about tourism does the writer mention?

Is Tourism Bad for the Environment?

Most people feel that their jobs are becoming more and more stressful. They work extremely hard, and don't have enough time to relax. It's no surprise that people want their holidays to be perfect. Many people look for continuous sunshine on the most luxurious beaches.

As a result, more people than ever travel to far-away countries to get that all-day sun. Moreover, travelling has also become safer and more comfortable. All of this has brought business and opportunities to many tourist destinations. The extra money this is bringing in can be used to develop health and education in these countries.

However, tourism has not been good news for the environment. First of all, transporting millions of tourists to their holiday resorts every year pollutes the air and the seas. Secondly, more and more hotels are built, and some of the world's most beautiful landscapes are destroyed forever. And finally, fresh water supplies are running low because of the extra demands for water.

To conclude, I think that tourism has a lot of negative consequences on nature. If we want our planet to be a healthy place, we need to travel less.

(b) Which words does the writer use to introduce each of the negative points?

(c) Match the underlined words with the words in the box.

> 1 on the other hand   2 to sum up   3 because of this
> 4 in addition

(d) Write your own composition about one of the following topics. Use topic sentences and remember to give both sides of the argument. Finish with your own opinion. Use the composition on tourism to help you. Write 120–180 words.

● Cars in cities – do we really need them?

● 'Bad boys on bikes' – should young people be forbidden to ride motorbikes?

For your portfolio

12 Mysterious places

* Indirect questions
* Modal verbs of deduction (past)
* Vocabulary: phrasal verbs
* Vocabulary: expressions with *be* + preposition

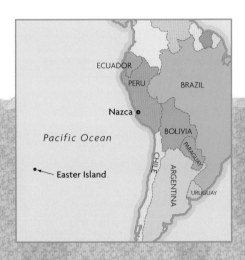

1 Read and listen

a Read the texts quickly and find two unanswered questions about each of the places.

No One Knows Why They're There

The world is full of wonderful places, both natural and man-made. Some of the man-made places are still unexplained. Here are two.

The Nazca Desert, Peru

The Nazca Desert is a high plain about 90 kilometres long and 8 kilometres wide on the coast of Peru, about 400 kilometres south of Lima. And it is covered in lines.

A long time ago, travellers in the Nazca Desert noticed the strange and obviously artificial lines on the ground. They wondered what the lines were and why they were there, but the lines were meaningless at ground level. Then, in the 20th century, people flew over the Nazca lines for the first time, and they realised that the lines formed special patterns. There are enormous figures of animals, people and plants – and lines that look similar to runways at modern airports.

It is known that these drawings are at least 1,500 years old. But no one is sure exactly when they were drawn, and, more importantly, no one knows *why* they were drawn. After all, why would anyone draw figures that you can only see from the air, in a period of history when there were no planes?

Easter Island

Easter Island, about halfway between Chile and Tahiti, is the world's most mysterious island. Discovered in 1722 by a Dutch explorer, Jacob Roggeveen, the island is famous for the *Moai*: hundreds of strange statues made from the island's volcanic rock, with faces that either look out to sea, or towards the local villages. Many have fallen over; some are incomplete. We don't really understand why they are there or who made them.

People still wonder how the statues were moved from where they were made to their present positions on the island. A writer called Erich von Däniken suggested that the *Moai* were built and moved by aliens. There are several other theories, but the answer has not yet been found.

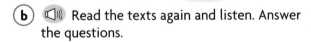

b 🔊 Read the texts again and listen. Answer the questions.

1 When and how did people first get an idea about what the Nazca lines are?

2 What do the lines show?

3 What are the *Moai* and what are they made of?

4 What was von Däniken's idea about the *Moai*?

Discussion box

Work in pairs or small groups. Discuss these questions together.

1 Do you think von Däniken's idea about Easter Island is right or wrong?

2 What other explanations can you think of for these places?

3 What other mysterious places do you know about?

2 Grammar

Indirect questions

(a) Which of these questions are direct? Which are indirect? Write *direct questions* and *indirect questions* above the lists.

We'd like to know why the lines are there.

People still wonder how the statues were moved.

Why are the lines there?

How were the statues moved?

(b) What is the word order after the question words in:

1   direct questions?   2   indirect questions?

(c) Circle the correct options.

1   I don't understand *why you are angry / why are you angry.*
2   I wonder *what is he doing / what he's doing.*
3   I don't know *where he is / where is he.*
4   I can't tell you *where has she gone / where she has gone.*
5   Nobody knows *who is he/ who he is.*

(d) Put the words in the correct order to make sentences.

1   know / we / it / where / is / don't
    We don't know where it is ------------------ .
2   wonder / who / man / I / that / is
    ------------------------------ .
3   you / tell / I / where / can't / are / they
    ------------------------------ .
4   is / we / understand / what / saying / don't / she
    ------------------------------ .

Indirect questions and auxiliaries

(e) Match the questions to the pictures. Write 1–4 in the boxes.

1   What time do you close?
2   When does it finish?
3   Where did you get that cold drink?
4   Did they win?

(f) 🔊 Listen and complete the questions that the people in the pictures in Exercise 2c asked.

1   Can you tell me what
    ------------------ ?
2   Do you know when ------------------ ?
3   Can you tell me where
    ------------------ ?
4   Do you know if ------------------ ?

(g) What happens to the auxiliary verbs after the question words in the indirect questions in Exercise 2f?

(h) Rewrite the questions.

1   'What does she do?'
    'Do you know what she does?'
2   'Where did they go?'
    'Can you tell me ------------------ ?'
3   'Does he live around here?'
    'Do you know ------------------ ?'
4   'What time does the plane leave?'
    'Can you tell me ------------------ ?'
5   'Does he speak English?'
    'Could you tell me ------------------ ?'

3 Speak

Write four indirect questions beginning with *Do you know ...* or *Can you tell me ... .*
Then work with a partner. Ask and answer the questions.

A: *Do you know where Easter Island is?*

B: *Yes, it's in the Pacific Ocean. Can you tell me who the first man on the moon was?*

4 Speak and listen

a Look at picture 1. This is a famous place in Britain. What is it called? What do you know about it?

b Now look at picture 2. In pairs or small groups, discuss the following questions.

1 Do you know what the structure is?
2 How old do you think it is?
3 What do you think it was used for?

c 🔊 Listen and complete the notes.

Seahenge

● Location:
  Norfolk, in the east of England

● Shape:
  ....

● Made of:
  ....

● Height:
  ....

● Age:
  ....

● Possible use of the site:
  ....

d 🔊 Listen again and mark the statements *T* (true) or *F* (false). Correct the false statements.

1 Seahenge is the same as Stonehenge. ☐
2 Seahenge was built in the water. ☐
3 We know exactly what Seahenge was used for. ☐
4 Visitors can go to the beach to see Seahenge. ☐
5 Seahenge can help us learn about people's lives in the past. ☐

5 Grammar

Modal verbs of deduction (past)

a Look at the examples.

1 They **must have built** the circle perhaps a kilometre or more from the coast.
2 They **can't/couldn't have built** Seahenge in the water.
3 People **might have put** the bodies of the dead on the tree in the middle.

Which one means:

a It is possible that this happened in the past?
b I'm sure this happened in the past?
c I'm sure this did not happen in the past?

> **Rule:** To make guesses about the .... , we use *must, might* (*not*), *can't* or *could* (*not*) + *have* + ...

b Complete the rule with *past participle* and *past*.

c Complete the sentences. Use modals of deduction and the correct form of the verb. There may be more than one possible answer.

1 Jane left without saying a word. She _must have been_ (be) very angry.
2 We don't know exactly where they got the trees from, but they .... (not bring) them here from somewhere far away. They're too heavy.
3 They recently found an ancient site in Peru. It's almost 3000 years old and it .... (be) a religious site, but we can't be sure.
4 I had my wallet an hour ago, but now I don't know where it is. I .... (leave) it in that shop!
5 Sally hasn't called me. She .... (not get) my text message.
6 Somebody .... (take) the book from her bag. Or maybe she left it on the bus.

6 Pronunciation

have in *must have / might have / can't have / couldn't have*

🔊 Turn to page 121.

7 Vocabulary

Phrasal verbs

(a) When did Howard Carter discover Tutankhamen's tomb? Read the article quickly to find out.

(b) Read the article again and match the underlined words with the definitions.

1 persuade (someone)
2 cancel
3 find (often by accident)
4 die
5 connect with (something)
6 begin (to describe someone's first profession)
7 stop shining or burning
8 be successful (when an effort is rewarded)

(c) Use three of the phrasal verbs to complete the sentences.

A: 'My grandmother _____ two months ago.'

B: 'I'm sorry to hear that.'

A: 'Thanks. Anyway, I was in her house looking through some of her papers when I _____ an unpaid electricity bill from 1966!'

B: 'So?'

A: 'Well, at the exact moment I found the bill, all the lights in the house _____ .'

B: 'Now, that is strange.'

(d) Work with a partner. Use three of the phrasal verbs to write a short dialogue.

THE CURSE OF TUTANKHAMEN'S TOMB

Howard Carter, perhaps the most famous archaeologist of all time, started out as an artist and in 1891 he set off for Egypt to paint the pyramids. However, he soon became Head Inspector of Upper Egypt Monuments.

In 1908 he met Lord Carnarvon, who put up the money for Carter's biggest dream – the search for Tutankhamen's tomb. However, in 1922 Carnarvon wanted to call off the expedition. He was beginning to believe the tomb would never be found. Carter talked him into continuing the search and on 4 November, 1922 Carter's hard work paid off. Finally, he stood at the entrance to the tomb.

With the discovery came stories of a curse. Above the entrance to the tomb Carter came across an inscription – 'Death Shall Come on Swift Wings To Him Who Disturbs the Peace of the King'. A few months later Carnarvon passed away after being bitten by an insect. At exactly the same time as he died all the lights in Cairo went out. It was the first of several mysterious deaths tied in with the discovery of the tomb.

8 Speak and listen

a) Match the underlined words with the definitions.

1 I found an old coin <u>buried</u> in the garden.
2 There's a secret <u>passageway</u> which leads to the garden.
3 My grandmother's got hundreds of <u>ornaments</u> in her house.
4 He said his love for me was <u>eternal</u>.
5 The priest gave me a <u>blessing</u>.
6 I saw a strange <u>apparition</u> in my bedroom last night.

a decorative objects
b forever
c hidden in the ground
d God's help and protection
e a ghost
f a narrow part of a building connecting two or more rooms

b) You are going to listen to part of a song called *The Curse of the Mummy's Tomb*. Work with a partner. Discuss how the words in Exercise 9a might be connected to the song.

The tomb must be buried in the ground.

c) 🔊 Listen to the song and write in the numbers of the missing lines.

1 There is writing on the wall
2 ~~In the Valley of the King,~~
3 Was this what you were afraid of?
4 And the king was on his way
5 There's no curse
6 It's up to you now

Did you know ...?

When World Party songwriter Karl Wallinger heard that superstar Robbie Williams was recording his song *She's the One* from his CD *Egyptology*, he was not very happy. However, Williams turned the song into a huge international hit and made Wallinger lots of money.

The Curse of the Mummy's Tomb
by World Party

Buried deep within the mountain,
a ___2___

There's a passageway that leads there,
Where the wind whistles and sings
Of a time so long forgotten
But it seems like yesterday
When the queen was in her palace
b _____

To the bosom of his family
To the holy golden womb
What was that love?
That's the curse of the mummy's tomb

If you want to know what happened here
c _____

There are strange signs and ornaments
That'll really tell you all
But they're easy to misunderstand
You have to tell the truth

That's how you find the secret
Of her eternal youth
There are curses that are blessings
There are clues in every room
d _____

That's the curse of the mummy's tomb

Nobody there to help you
As the apparition nears
Nobody loves like she did
Could take away your fears
e _____

Life without a queen
Forget it just remember
This life is but a dream
And you know that hope's returning
Like a new bride to the groom
f _____

Just a mummy's tomb

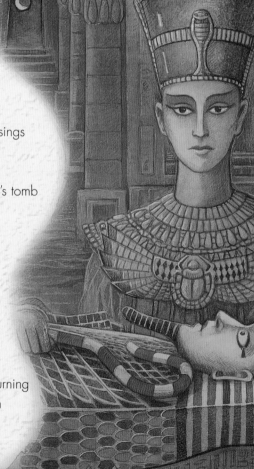

9 Vocabulary

Expressions with *be* + preposition

(a) Look at this line from the song and choose the best explanation.

It's up to you now

1 It's your fault   2 It's your responsibility   3 It's your destiny

(b) Here are some more expressions with *to be* + preposition. Match the two parts of the dialogues.

1   Let's go for a curry.

2   But you always let me copy your homework.

3   It's getting dark early today.

4   Why are you a vegetarian?

a   I'm against cruelty to animals.

b   I can't, I'm off hot food for a while.

c   Not anymore. I think the teacher's onto us.

d   Yeah, I think it's about to rain.

(c) Match the underlined expressions in Exercise 9b with the words.

1 is going to   2 don't like anymore   3 suspects   4 don't agree with

10 Write

(a) To get ideas for writing stories, ask yourself some questions and use the answers to develop the narrative.

Look at the story and find the answers to the writer's questions.

1   What did you see in the room?

2   You walked forward and looked behind the curtain and found something. What was it?

3   You heard a noise? What did you think it was? What did you do?

4   You looked down into your hands. What did you see?

(b) Think of four questions to help you write a story. Swap your questions with a partner. Answer their questions and use them to develop a story. Write 120–180 words.

I was standing in the doorway of a large room. I didn't know where I was or how I got here. It was a large empty room. There was hardly anything in it – no chairs, no tables, no cupboards. The only piece of furniture was a large mirror. It was broken and there was glass all over the floor. At the far end of the room was a window. There was a curtain drawn across it.

I decided to open the curtains to let more light into the room but when I got there my foot kicked against something hard on the floor. I looked down and saw a foot sticking out from under the curtains. It was then that I noticed the blood – it was everywhere.

Suddenly I heard the sound of police cars. There must have been hundreds of them. I panicked but I didn't know why. I hadn't done anything wrong.

Then I looked down into my hands and I saw it – the knife, its shiny blade dripping with blood ...

For your portfolio

Module 3 Check your progress

1 Grammar

a Complete the sentences. Use the gerund or infinitive form of the verb.

1 I can't afford _to buy_ (buy) the new U2 CD this month.
2 I want _____ (be) a rock star.
3 She hopes _____ (travel) around South America before she goes to university.
4 I've decided _____ (study) engineering at university.
5 I don't really feel like _____ (go) out tonight. Let's wait until tomorrow.
6 Did you remember _____ (give) Jenny a birthday present?
7 I don't mind _____ (get) up early during the week, but not at the weekend.
8 Sorry I'm late. I stopped _____ (have) a coffee.
9 I stopped _____ (drink) coffee 2 years ago.

[ ] 8

b Write *I wish* sentences.

1 'My computer's too slow.'
   I wish I had a faster computer.
2 'I'm too short.'
   _____
3 'I don't understand physics.'
   _____
4 'My football team are bottom of the league.'
   _____

[ ] 3

c Complete the sentences. Use the correct form of the second conditional.

1 If I _lived_ (live) by the beach I _would go_ (go) surfing everyday.
2 If we _____ (have) a bigger house I _____ (not share) a bedroom with my brother.
3 She _____ (be) healthier if she _____ (do) some exercise.
4 We _____ (not be) lost if we _____ (have) a map.
5 If he _____ (not talk) so quickly, I _____ (understand) him better.
6 _____ you _____ (travel) around the world if you _____ (win) lots of money?

[ ] 5

d Make one sentence, using the linker at the end. Sometimes there is more than one possibility.

1 I don't usually like romance films. I enjoyed *Love Actually*. **(although)** _Although I don't usually like romantic films, I enjoyed_ Love Actually.
2 He's not very tall. He plays basketball really well. **(despite)** _____
3 I look like my mother. My brother looks like my father. **(however)** _____
4 I continued working. I was really tired. **(even though)** _____
5 I thought the exam was difficult. I think I passed. **(although)** _____

[ ] 4

e Rewrite the questions.

1 What time does the film start?
   Do you know _what time the film starts?_
2 Where did they go?
   Can you tell me _____
3 Did she leave her phone number?
   Do you know _____
4 Does she like me?
   Do you know _____
5 Who won the game?
   Can you tell me _____

[ ] 4

f Circle the correct words.

1 She won the competition. She (must be) / can't be a good singer.
2 I saw them ten minutes ago, so they *must have gone / can't have gone* far.
3 They're speaking Spanish, so they *might be / can't be* from Argentina.
4 I rang her but she didn't answer. She *might have gone / can't have gone* to bed early.
5 You've just eaten. You *can't be / might be* hungry already!
6 Their house looks very dark. They *could be / could have been* on holiday.

[ ] 5

2 Vocabulary

a) Complete the sentences. Use the correct form of the verbs in the box.

look	come	~~make~~	let	turn	hook
get	hang				

1 *Make* up your mind. Do you want an ice-cream or not?
2 I have lots of friends that I .... out with.
3 They offered me more money to work on Thursday evenings but I .... them down.
4 I really .... up to my brother. He's such a great guy.
5 I'm coming to London next week. Do you want to .... up?
6 I've .... up with a great idea for making money!
7 I promise to do a good job. I won't .... you down.
8 I hate rainy Monday mornings. They really .... me down.

[7]

b) Underline the odd one out in each group and say why it doesn't belong.

1 relate to   hook up with   slow down   hang out with
2 burglary   excitement   shoplifting   vandalism
3 law   prison   fine   community service
4 sort out   call off   think over   sleep on
5 entertain   agree   kind   enjoy

[5]

c) Complete the sentences. Use the correct form of the word at the end.

1 This is a great meal and it doesn't need a lot of *preparation* . PREPARE
2 He has the perfect .... for writing stories. IMAGINE
3 Going to the cinema is my favourite form of .... ENTERTAIN
4 I never realised my .... was so great in the UK. POPULAR
5 I always remember my grandmother for her .... KIND
6 From his .... , I don't think he was very happy. REACT
7 There's a .... I can't come to your party but I'm not sure yet. POSSIBLE

8 Yoga is a great form of .... RELAX

[7]

d) Write the correct word in each space.

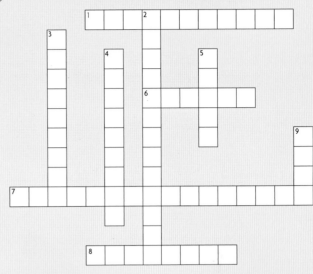

Across

1 Taking goods from a shop without paying for them.
6 A building where criminals live as a punishment.
7 Work which criminals are sometimes ordered to do (2 words).
8 The crime of illegally entering a building and stealing things.

Down

2 Stealing things out of pockets or bags, especially in a crowd.
3 The crime of damaging other people's property.
4 The crime of stealing a car and driving fast and dangerously for fun.
5 The crime of starting a fire in order to damage a building.
9 Money that has to be paid as a punishment for breaking the law.

[9]

How did you do?

Tick (✓) a box for each section.

Total score:	☺ Very good	☺ OK	☹ Not very good
[57]	Very good	OK	Not very good
Grammar	23 – 29	15 – 22	less than 15
Vocabulary	22 – 28	14 – 21	less than 14

Module 4
Emotions

YOU WILL LEARN ABOUT ...

- A love story from 1906 ....
- Different wedding ceremonies ....
- Getting angry ....
- *The Lord of the Rings* ....
- Scary films ....
- What makes people happy ....

✳ **Can you match each picture with a topic?**

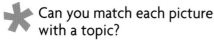

YOU WILL LEARN HOW TO ...

Speak
- Talk about giving and receiving presents
- Describe someone's appearance
- Describe someone's personality
- Talk about weddings in your country
- Talk about something you regret doing
- Talk about things that make you angry
- Discuss scary films
- Discuss ghosts and ghost stories
- Talk about your idea of happiness

Write
- A description of a person you know
- A story about getting angry
- A film review
- A poem

Read
- A story about a special present
- An article about different wedding ceremonies
- Short texts from a website
- An article about *The Lord of the Rings* and its author
- An extract from a ghost story
- An article about happiness

Listen
- A description of the film *The English Patient*
- Stories about getting angry
- A description of the film *The Blair Witch Project*
- Dialogues about being happy
- A song

Use grammar

Can you match the names of the grammar points with the examples?

Reporting verbs	Why don't you **sort** the problem **out**?
Third conditional	I **used to live** in Tokyo, so I'**m used to speaking** Japanese.
I wish / if only + past perfect simple	Elijah, **who played Frodo**, was only 18 at the time.
should have / shouldn't have	We **shouldn't have spent** all the money.
Non-defining relative clauses	She **offered** to pay, but I **told** her not to worry about it.
Defining relative clauses	I **wish I had got up** earlier this morning.
be used to + gerund vs. *used to* + infinitive	James Bond is a secret agent **whose** codename is 007.
Grammar of phrasal verbs	If you **hadn't told** me, I **would have forgotten**.

Use vocabulary

Can you think of two more examples for each topic?

Appearance	Personality	Phrasal verbs with *out*	Adjectives with prefixes
curly hair	sensitive	work something out	polite/impolite
moustache	independent	look out	usual/unusual
....	....	....	....
....	....	....	....

13 Love

* Reported speech review
* Reporting verbs
* Vocabulary: appearance
* Vocabulary: personality

1 Read and listen

(a) Tell your partner about a love story that you really liked or disliked. What other kinds of stories do you like?

(b) Look at the pictures. What do you think the story will be about? Read the story quickly to check your ideas.

(c) 🔊 Read the text again and listen. Answer the questions.

1 What does the story tell us about the way Della and Jim live?

2 Why do you think Della took a deep breath before she went into the second shop?

3 Why do you think Jim gasped in surprise when Della came out of the bedroom?

4 Why do you think Della gave Jim his present a day early?

5 Why do you think Jim smiled when he opened the present that Della gave him?

6 How do you think Jim got the money for the hair clasp?

Discussion box

Work in pairs or small groups. Discuss these questions together.

1 Do you think this is a happy story, or a sad one?

2 What's the best/worst present you've ever received?

3 What's the best present you've ever given?

The Gift of the Magi

(a story by O. Henry – adapted)

It was the day before Christmas. James and Della's first as a married couple. Early in the morning, Della said goodbye to James as he left their tiny flat for work. He turned round, smiled at her and stroked her long, straight brown hair. He wasn't broad-shouldered, or very good-looking, in fact he was kind of short and plump, but he was her 'Jim' – poor, maybe, but she loved him because he was kind, patient and generous. 'I love that hair!' said Jim (as he always did), and then Della went inside.

Della took out her purse. In it was one dollar and eighty-seven cents. It was all she had in the world, and she felt like crying – not because they didn't have enough to eat (they were poor, but not that poor) but because she wanted to buy Jim a really special Christmas present – but with less than two dollars?

Della went into town. She stopped to look in the jeweller's window. There was the silver hair clasp she'd always wanted, and then she saw a beautiful gold watch-chain. That was it! Jim had a watch, his favourite possession: it had been his father's, but it didn't have a chain. She went in and asked how much the chain was. Five dollars! She walked out, almost in tears. How was she going to find the rest of the money?

As she walked sadly down the street she saw a sign outside another shop: 'We buy hair'. She looked at her long hair in her reflection in the window. She took a deep breath and went in.

Jim came home that evening, whistling happily. In his hand was the present he'd bought for Della. He went in the flat and called her name. He gasped in surprise when Della came out of the bedroom, her hair cropped short and spiky. She ran to him and asked him not to be angry with her, and then she said 'I can't wait until tomorrow. I must give you it immediately. Happy Christmas!' and gave him his present. Jim unwrapped it, smiled and sat down. Then Della told him why she'd had her hair cut off: 'I sold my hair to buy the chain. Jim – why are you smiling like that? Don't you like your present?'

Jim looked at her. 'It's wonderful – and I'm still in love with you, with or without the hair. But look, here's your present.' Della didn't know what to think when she saw – the silver hair clasp. 'Oh Jim, thank you – and it's OK, I can grow my hair again. But … how did you get the money for this?'

Jim smiled again. 'Let's just put our presents away, Della, and have dinner. I'll tell you about it later.'

2 Grammar

Reported statements review

(a) Match the two parts of the sentences.

1 She went in and asked
2 She asked him
3 Della told him

a not to be angry with her.
b why she'd had her hair cut off.
c how much the chain was.

(b) Look at the examples. What happens to the verb in reported speech?

'I *bought* my girlfriend a present,' said Tom. ➔ Tom said he'*d bought* his girlfriend a present.

'It *didn't cost* a lot,' said Tom. ➔ Tom said it *hadn't cost* a lot.

(c) Write the reported speech.

1 'I love your hair,' Jim said. _Jim said that he loved her hair._ .
2 'I sold my hair,' said Della. _____ .
3 'I must give you it immediately,' she said. _____ .
4 'I've bought a present for you,' said Jim. _____ .
5 'I can grow my hair again,' she said. _____ .
6 'I won't stop loving you,' He said. _____ .

Reported questions review

(d) With reported questions we use the word order of a statement and not a question. It is important to see what kind of question is being reported.

> **Rule:**
>
> - With *yes/no* questions we use *if* or *whether* and the same word order as a statement.
>   'Are you enjoying the party?' ➔ She asked me if/whether I was enjoying the party.
> - With *wh-* question words we use the same word order as a statement.
>   'What's your favourite colour?' ➔ She asked me what my favourite colour was.
>   'Why didn't they come to my party?' ➔ He asked me why they hadn't come to his party.
> - With requests we use *asked* + person + infinitive
>   'Can you help me, Ali?' asked Nick. ➔ Nick asked Ali to help him.
>   'Can you not smoke, please?' ➔ Paul asked Liz not to smoke.

(e) Put the questions into reported speech.

> We asked readers to send in questions that famous people might have asked! Here are some of your ideas:
>
> 1 Columbus: 'Is this the right way to India?'
>   _Columbus asked if it was the right way to India._
>
> 2 Neil Armstrong: 'Can I go first?'
>   _____ .
>
> 3 William Shakespeare: 'Where's my pen?'
>   _____ .
>
> 4 Walt Disney: 'What name can I give to this mouse?'
>   _____ .
>
> 5 Ellen McArthur: 'When will I sail around the world again?'
>   _____ .

3 Vocabulary and speaking

Appearance

a Read through the text in Exercise 1 and underline physical descriptions of Della and Jim.

a moustache   straight   a double chin   ~~wavy~~
broad-shouldered   wrinkles   cropped   a ponytail
highlights   a tattoo   long   spots   ~~slim~~
an afro   a centre parting   ~~a scar~~   long eyelashes
a fringe   short   a beard   medium height   rosy cheeks
tall   plump   well-built   freckles   bushy eyebrows
~~clean-shaven~~   a mole   spiky

b Put the words in the box in the correct columns in the table. Use the pictures to help you.

face	hair	height and build	special features
clean-shaven	wavy	slim	a scar

c Work in pairs. Student A describes a famous person to Student B, using the language in Exercise 3b. Student B listens and guesses who it is. Swap roles.

Personality

d Make a list of words you know to describe someone's personality: *friendly*, *honest* ...

e Here are other words about personality. Complete the definitions.

bossy   considerate   sensible   determined   sensitive   insensitive
bad-tempered   ~~ambitious~~   imaginative   independent

1   A person who wants to be successful, powerful or wealthy is *ambitious* .
2   A person who doesn't care about or doesn't notice other people's feelings is _____ .
3   A person who is easily upset by what other people do or say *or* a person who understands what other people need and is helpful and kind to them is _____ .
4   A person who does things by themselves without help from others is _____ .
5   A person who has lots of creative ideas is _____ .
6   A person who has good judgement is _____ .
7   A person who has a strong desire to do something and who doesn't let others stop them, is _____ .
8   A person who becomes angry very easily, often without a real reason, is _____ .
9   A person who always tells others what to do is _____ .
10   A person who always thinks about what other people need is _____ .

4 Speak

Work with a partner.

1   Describe the appearance of the oldest and the youngest person in your family.
2   Think of different people in your family. How are their personalities similar or different?

5 Listen

a 🔊 Listen to a conversation about the film *The English Patient* and put the pictures in the correct order. Write 1–5 in the boxes.

b 🔊 Complete the sentences with the verbs in the box. Then listen again and check.

| tells   explains   agrees   begs   suggests |

1 He .... her that he has to leave her to get help.
2 He .... taking her to a cave that he knows.
3 He also .... that it will be at least three days before he'll be back.
4 She .... to stay in the cave.
5 He .... them to help him, but they refuse.

6 Grammar
Reporting verbs

a Complete the rule with the verbs in the box.

| agree   beg   explain   persuade   suggest |

> **Rule:**
> - *offer, refuse,* .... + infinitive with *to*:
>   I **offered to help** you with your work.
> - *say,* .... + *that* + clause:
>   She **said that she'd call me**.
> - *apologise for,* .... + gerund:
>   They **apologised for being** so noisy.
> - *ask, order, invite, tell,* .... , ...
>   + object + infinitive with *to*:
>   He **asked me to give** him some money.

b Rewrite the sentences in reported speech. Use the correct reporting verb.

1 'Can you phone me at 7 o'clock?' the boy said to her.
   The boy asked her to phone him at 7 o'clock.
2 'I broke a glass. I'm so sorry,' she said.
3 'Oh, please, please write to me!' he said to her.
4 'I can help you with your emails,' I said.
5 'I haven't got my homework because the dog ate it,' said the student.
6 'Go out into the garden!' she said to the boys.
7 'I'm not going to help you,' he said.

7 Pronunciation
Intonation in reported questions

🔊 Turn to page 121.

Culture in mind

8 Read

(a) What do these people do at a wedding?

> bride   bridegroom (groom)   best man   priest   witnesses

(b) Read the magazine article and answer the questions.

At which wedding:

1 does the groom give the bride a present?
2 do the bride and groom walk around a fire?
3 does the bride have powder in her hair?

(c) Write six questions about the article to test your partner.

Wedding Ceremonies

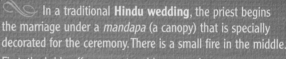 The style of an **Islamic wedding** varies, depending on the cultural background of the couple, but the process is very simple. There are two ceremonies.

The first is the *Nikkah* ceremony. This could be in a mosque, at the bride's or groom's house, or at the house of the man who conducts the ceremony – an *Imam*. The groom must give the bride a gift, known as *mahr*, in order to allow the marriage. Both the bride and groom must decide and agree on the value and nature of the mahr – this could be something simple like a copy of the *Qur'an* (the holy book of Islam), or large amounts of money, jewellery or houses. Permission for the marriage must be given by both the bride and groom in front of witnesses, and they are declared man and wife. Although there are no special clothes, the bride usually covers her head with the *hijab* (Muslim headscarf) and the groom often wears a small cap. The *Nikkah* will often include readings from the *Qur'an* and prayers to ask God to bless the couple.

The second part of an Islamic wedding is the *Walima* – a party given by the groom. It could be immediately after the *Nikkah* ceremony or several months later. Friends and relatives are invited to share a meal and celebrate the marriage. The men and women usually sit separately. A *Walima* could be a small homemade meal for ten guests or a grand occasion in a hotel with hundreds of people.

In a traditional **Hindu wedding**, the priest begins the marriage under a *mandapa* (a canopy) that is specially decorated for the ceremony. There is a small fire in the middle.

First, the bride offers yogurt and honey to the groom as a token of purity and sweetness. Then she spreads turmeric powder on her hands to accept her change of status from an unmarried woman to a wife. Her father pours out some sacred water to symbolise the 'giving away' of the daughter to the bridegroom.

The bride and the bridegroom face each other, and the priest ties their clothes together and they put a ring of flowers around each other's neck and exchange their rings.

Then the bridegroom stands facing west and the bride sits in front of him facing east; they hold hands and say prayers for happiness and a long life together. Then, holding hands, they walk around the fire three times.

Satapadi is the most important part of the ceremony. Here the bride and the bridegroom take seven steps together around the fire and make seven promises to each other. The ceremony finishes with a prayer that the marriage will never end. They are now husband and wife. The groom places *sindhoor* (a red powder) on the bride's hair to show she is a married woman. The groom's parents bless the couple and offer cloth or flowers to the bride and the families throw flowers on the couple and bless them.

Discussion box

Work in pairs or small groups. Discuss these questions together.

1 What happens at a traditional wedding in your country?
2 Have you been to a wedding from a different culture? What happened?

9 Vocabulary
Relationships

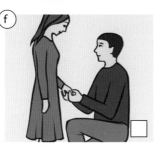

(a) Match the phrases with the pictures. Write 1–6 in the boxes.

> Oliver met Isabel when he was 19 and they started ¹going out. After a year they ²got engaged, but then they had a big argument and Jill ³broke up with him. Then they ⁴got back together and got married. They were married for twelve years, but then they ⁵got divorced. And now Oliver ⁶has fallen in love with someone else!

(b) Use the phrases in the box to complete the sentences.

> are getting divorced   going out   get married
> got engaged   broken up   get back together
> fell in love

1 Did you know? James is _____ with Becky.
2 Amy met and _____ with Jon at university.
3 It's really sad that so many married people _____ these days.
4 My sister has _____ to a French guy – they're going to _____ next year.
5 It's a pity that Joe and Amber have _____ – I hope they _____ again soon.

10 Write

(a) Read the composition and answer the questions. Which paragraph:

1 describes her personality, and mentions something to illustrate it?
2 says who the person was and how the writer knew them?
3 says how the writer has changed through what they learned from that person?
4 describes the person's appearance?

The person who has taught me the most about life is my grandmother. My parents did a lot of travelling when I was younger so I spent most of my school holidays with her. She was more than just a grandmother to me and when she died a few years ago I felt I'd lost a really good friend.

She always looked really good for her age. She had wavy grey hair and a big round face with really rosy cheeks. She was always smiling. She wasn't very tall and she was a little plump.

She was such a considerate person. She knew how much I missed my parents so she did everything she could to make me feel at home. She was also really imaginative and spent hours telling me stories that she had made up. I'm sure it was because of her that I became a writer.

But as well as keeping a young boy entertained, she taught me so many important things. I was very impatient when I was a child and she taught me that good things happened if you could wait for them. She was such a positive person and she also taught me how to look for the good in everything.

(b) Think of a person who has taught you something important. Write your own composition about them. Use the composition above to help you. Write 120–180 words.

For your portfolio

14) Anger

* Third conditional review
* *I wish / if only* for past situations
* *should have / shouldn't have (done)*
* Vocabulary: anger

1 Read and listen

(a) Read the text. Who is Barry Cadish and what does he do?

(b) Read the texts and match them with the titles. Write 1–4 in the boxes. There is one title you do not need to use.

1   A missed opportunity
2   Mum and Dad know best
3   Never talk to strangers
4   Beauty is only skin deep

What would you do differently if you had a second chance? What have you learned from your decisions? What advice do you have for others who may face similar choices? In 1999 Barry Cadish launched his website, **regretsonly.com**. Barry encouraged people to send in their regrets and share them on the Web. The idea was so popular that Barry published a book of hundreds of the regrets he had received.

☐ CJ, 31, social worker

I wish I had given the plain-looking guys a second chance while I was at school. I always went for handsome, athletic types. So, where am I today? Married to a good-looking idiot. A handsome man who has no heart, no compassion, and no love for anyone but himself.

I sometimes visit my family back in my home town and occasionally I run into old classmates – the plain-looking guys. And what do I see now? Very intelligent, warm, funny men who are everything I want, but will never have in a husband.

☐ Mia, 22, photographer

When I was at school I played in most of the school sports teams. I remember one year our football team had to win the last game to get into the finals. Three minutes of the game left and we needed to score. I got control of the ball and ran towards the goal.
Our captain was right next to me shouting 'go on, take a shot'. But I panicked and passed the ball to her. She shot and missed. If only I hadn't passed the ball.

I knew immediately that if I had taken the shot I would have scored. Ever since that game I've always taken every opportunity I could.

☐ Ben, 52, mechanic

I wish I had listened to my parents more when I was a teenager. Thinking back, they gave me lots of good advice but I ignored everything they said. I thought they were old and didn't know anything. Now I have got two teenagers of my own, I realise how right they were.

If I had listened to them, I might have made some better decisions in my life. I would have gone to university and probably waited a bit before I got married. I hope my daughters will listen to me more than I listened to my parents.

(c) 🔊 Read the texts again and listen. Answer the questions.

1   Who is unhappily married?
2   Who used their experience to change their life?
3   Who has children?
4   Who has a regret about when they were a teenager?
5   Who regrets a single action?

Discussion box

Work in pairs or small groups. Discuss these questions together.

1   Do you think this is a good idea for a website? Why / Why not?

2   Have you got a story you could send to the site? Tell your partner.

2 Grammar

Third conditional review

(a) Read the examples and answer the questions. Then complete the rules.

*If I **had taken** the shot, I **would have scored**.*

1 Did Mia take a shot? Did she score?

*If I **had listened** to them, I **might have made** some better decisions in my life.*

2 Did Ben listen to his parents? Did he make the best decisions for his life?

> **Rule:**
> - To speculate how past actions and results might have been different we use *if* + _____ and *would* + _____ .
> - We use *would* (for certainty) and _____ (for uncertainty).

(b) Tom is a Norwich City football fan. His wife Josie is a doctor. How do you think they met?

Join the sentences, using the third conditional, to check your ideas.

1 Norwich got to the final.

2 Tom wanted to watch the game on TV.

If Norwich hadn't got to the final, Tom wouldn't have wanted to watch the game on TV.

3 He found out the TV wasn't working.

If Tom hadn't wanted to watch the game ...

4 He climbed on the roof to check the aerial.

5 He fell off the roof.

6 He went to hospital.

7 He met a doctor called Josie.

8 He fell in love with her and got married.

(c) Think about five things you did or didn't do which had an effect on your life. Write down the first clause of a third conditional sentence for each one.

If I hadn't gone to the disco last weekend ...
If I had studied harder for the history test ...

Read your partner's sentences and guess how they finish.

If you hadn't gone to the disco last weekend, you wouldn't have met your new boyfriend.

3 Grammar

I wish / if only for past situations

(a) Look at the examples from the text, answer the questions and complete the rule.

*I **wish I had given** the plain-looking guys a second chance while I was at school.*

*If only **I hadn't passed** the ball.*

*I **wish I had listened** to my parents more when I was a teenager.*

1 Was CJ interested in plain guys at school? Did Mia keep the ball? Did Ben listen to his parents?

2 How do CJ, Mia and Ben feel about these past actions – happy or sad?

> **Rule:**
> - To express regret about past actions we use *wish* or *if only* with the _____ tense.

(b) Write sentences using *wish* or *if only* and your own ideas.

1 *I wish I hadn't gone to bed so late last night.*
I'm really tired today.

2 _____
I'm so hungry.

3 _____
I'll never find another girl like her.

4 _____
I've got a really bad headache.

5 _____
How am I going to tell my parents?

6 _____
Where am I going to find another one?

4 Listen

a Work with a partner. There are two stories in the six pictures. What are they? Tell your stories to another pair.

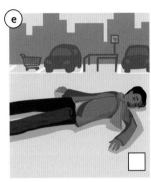

b 🔊 Listen to the stories and check your ideas. Put the pictures in the correct order. Write 1–7 in the boxes. One picture is used in both stories.

c 🔊 Listen again to the first story and choose the correct answer.

1 The storyteller:
   a was shopping at the time
   b heard the story from a friend
   c was watching a Christmas film

2 The two women were arguing about the turkey because:
   a of how much it cost
   b they both wanted to pay for it
   c they both wanted to buy it

3 After one woman had paid for the turkey:
   a they both left the shop
   b the other woman bought a chicken
   c they started shouting in the shop

4 At first, most people watching were:
   a horrified
   b amused
   c not paying any attention

5 One woman hit the other with:
   a her hand
   b her shopping bag
   c the turkey

6 In the end:
   a one woman drove away
   b both women went to hospital
   c someone stopped the fight

5 Speak

a Work with a partner. Look at the items in the box below, then discuss the questions.

> mobile phones going off in the cinema
>
> queuing up for fast food
>
> not being able to watch what you want on TV
>
> parents wanting to know who you're going out with and what time you're going to be back
>
> the behaviour of your best friends

1 Do any of the things in the box make you angry?

2 What do you do in these situations?

3 What other situations make you or members of your family angry?

4 What about when you were younger? Have you changed?

6 Grammar

should have / shouldn't have (done)

a (Circle) the correct meaning of these lines from the two stories, then complete the rule.

1   Yes, I know what you're thinking – I shouldn't have done that.
    She did it. / She didn't do it.

2   I should've just gone to a shop and bought another drink.
    He went. / He didn't go.

b Match the two parts of the sentences.

1	I should go to the shop	a	because I don't have time.
2	I should have gone to the shop	b	before it closed.
3	I shouldn't go to the shop	c	because I spent too much money.
4	I shouldn't have gone to the shop	d	before it closes.

c Work with a partner. Write responses to these statements using *should've / shouldn't have.* Practise with your partner.

A: *I can't believe they didn't pick me for the team.*
B: *Well, you should've trained harder.*

1   I didn't have enough money to buy it.
2   I got a zero for my homework.
3   I left the oven on and burnt the pizza.
4   My best friend's not talking to me.
5   She lent him €100 and he lost it.
6   I have to go the dentist again tomorrow.

7 Pronunciation

should have / shouldn't have

🔊 Turn to page 121.

8 Vocabulary

Anger

a Read the text and complete the definitions with the underlined words.

1   quite angry – be __*cross*__ with someone

2   someone who gets angry really quickly – they are ....

3   get angry – lose your ....

4   a sudden and long display of anger (usually from a young child) – have a ....

5   get angry really suddenly and shout at someone – bite someone's ....

6   not get angry – keep your ....

7   really, really angry – be .... with someone

8   not angry – be ....

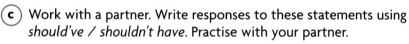

My angry family

My dad's <u>furious</u> with me. I took his car without asking. He really <u>lost his temper</u>.

My mum's <u>cross</u> with me because I forgot to buy some milk on my way home from school.

My sister's just <u>bitten my head off</u> because I talked during her soap opera. She's so <u>hot-headed</u>.

My baby brother's having <u>a tantrum</u> because he wants some ice cream.

I'm the only one who's <u>calm</u>. Up here all alone in my bedroom, I'm the only one who knows how to <u>keep their cool</u>.

b Work with a partner and discuss the questions.

1   When was the last time you were furious with someone, and why?

2   What kind of things do your parents get cross with you for?

3   Did you have tantrums when you were a child?

Working things out

9 Read and listen

(a) 🔊 Does Matt still have a problem with the motorbike?
What offer does Ben make? Read, listen and check your answers.

Matt: Hi, Tony. Can I talk to you for a moment?

Tony: Well, it's young Matt. You've been keeping out of my way, haven't you? I hope you're here to pay me the rest of the money you owe me.

Matt: Well, the thing is, I haven't got it.

Tony: Then we've got a bit of a problem, haven't we?

Matt: Well, what I mean is, I haven't got the money right now – so I was hoping we could sort something out, so I can pay you later. Next month, perhaps?

Tony: Oh yeah? And how do I know you'll pay me next month?

Joanne: He will.

Tony: And who are you?

Joanne: I'm Joanne, his girlfriend, and I know Matt's really honest. If he says he'll pay you, then he will.

Ben: Yeah – and there's something I want to say, too. If Matt has any problem getting the money together, then I'll pay you instead of him.

Matt: Ben?

Tony: Well, in that case – yeah, OK. Let's make it next month. But make sure it is next month, OK?

Matt: Sure, Tony – no problem. Thanks.

Caroline: Hi guys – what's going on?

Joanne: We were just talking to Tony, the guy Matt bought the bike from. He's agreed to let Matt pay him back next month.

Caroline: That's great – I'm glad it's worked out so well.

Matt: And Ben – thanks a lot, mate. It was great of you to help me out like that – brilliant!

Joanne: Come on, we need to go and celebrate.

Caroline: Yes, let's – and Ben, it's good to have you back.

Ben: I'm glad to be back. Mates forever, eh?

(b) Answer the questions.

1 What does Tony hope when he sees Matt?

2 When does Matt want to pay Tony the money?

3 Why does Joanne promise Tony that Matt will pay the money?

4 What do Tony and Matt finally agree on?

5 Why do you think Caroline tells Ben that it's great to have him back?

10 Everyday English

(a) Find expressions 1–4 in the story. Who says them?

1 the thing is
2 what I mean is
3 there's something I want to say
4 in that case

Which one is used:

a to correct what you have said or say something in more detail? ☐

b to introduce a subject for discussion? ☐

c to talk about a situation that has already been mentioned? ☐

d to introduce a really important statement? ☐

(b) Use one of the phrases in each space.

1 There's no tea left? .... , I'll have orange juice.

2 .... , my parents like me to be home by midnight.

3 I really love him – .... , as a friend.

4 .... I can't go on holiday with you.

11 Write

(a) Read the story. What happened when the writer got home?

(b) Write a story about a time when you got angry. Use the vocabulary from Exercise 8 to help you. Write 120–180 words.

DANGER: JOGGERS!

A few years ago my wife and I were living in New York. Our apartment was next to Central Park, and every morning I went for a run before I went to work.

A lot of people had told me to be careful of muggers in the park, so I didn't usually take anything with me. But one morning my wife asked me to buy some bread on the way home, so I put $10 in my back pocket.

While I was running through the park, another jogger bumped into me. He apologised and continued running. I thought it was bit strange, so I checked my pocket and found that the money was missing. I immediately ran after the other jogger and grabbed him by his arm. I started shouting and demanding that he give me the $10. I'm not usually a hot-headed person but I really lost my temper. This frightened him and he quickly put his hand in his pocket and gave me the money. Then he ran away as fast as he could.

I bought the bread and went home. As soon as I got there, I began to tell my wife my story. 'You won't believe what happened to me!' I started. She immediately interrupted, 'I know, you left the money for the bread on the kitchen table.'

For your portfolio

15 Fear

* Defining and non-defining relative clauses
* Articles
* Vocabulary: adjectives with prefixes
* Vocabulary: phrasal verbs with *sit*

1 Read and listen

(a) Look at the photos. Which is your favourite character?

(b) Read the article and match the titles with the paragraphs. Write A–E in the boxes. There is one title you do not need to use.

A Afraid of fame

B Frodo – not just another superhero

C Elijah the hobbit

D The endless journey

E Success at the cinema

(c) 🔊 Read the article again and listen. Answer the questions.

1 Which one of these people or places is not real?

a Elijah Wood
b Middle Earth
c J.R.R. Tolkien
d Cedar Falls

2 Which of these were not Frodo's companions?

a dwarves   b elves
c angels   d humans

3 Which of these statements about *The Lord of the Rings* is not true?

a The films were made in New Zealand.

b The three films were all made together.

c It took three years to make the films.

d The books were written over 40 years ago.

THE FEAR IN ALL OF US

1 ☐ Surviving impossible situations is one of cinema's greatest themes; Charlie's Angels, James Bond, Indiana Jones and Frodo Baggins are all fictional heroes whose adventures are filled with unbelievable danger. But Frodo, whose quiet life changes when his uncle gives him a ring, is somehow different from Bond, Jones and the Angels. They always appear unafraid of what is coming after them. However, the hero of the enormously successful *The Lord of the Rings* shows fear in every little hobbit-step he takes.

2 ☐ This is part of the reason for the huge success of the movies, which were all filmed at the same time and shown each December between 2001 and 2003. Frodo faces the evil Sauron with his group of hobbits, elves, dwarves and humans. He is as frightened as we would be. The situations might be unrealistic, but the fear is not.

3 ☐ It was also fear that gave Elijah Wood his chance to become Frodo. The young actor, who was only 18 at the time, got the part by sending the director a video tape of himself running in a forest dressed as a hobbit. 'I wanted that part so badly, but I was too frightened to audition in person,' said Wood, born in Cedar Falls, USA. 'And Frodo is a hobbit who speaks with a British accent – so that's what I had to learn!' He was also afraid of spending so much time away in New Zealand, where the films were made over 18 months.

4 ☐ Fear also runs from the character and the actor to the author himself. J.R.R. Tolkien invented the land of Middle Earth, which was Frodo's home, in the 1950s. It was a place where Tolkien himself could feel safe. The writer, who died 30 years before the films appeared, hated the attention caused by the success of his books. He changed his telephone number and even moved house to escape the dozens of fans who came to find out more about his characters.

2 Grammar

Non-defining relative clauses (giving extra information)

(a) How are these sentences connected in the text? Is the information after or between the commas necessary to understand the rest of the sentence?

1 The young actor, ... was only 18 at the time, got the part by sending the director a video tape.

2 This is part of the reason for the huge success of the films, ... were all made at the same time.

3 He was also afraid of spending so much time away from home in New Zealand, ... the films were made.

4 Frodo, ... life changes when his uncle gives him a ring, is somehow different from Bond, Jones and the Angels.

(b) Complete the rule.

> **Rule:**
> - We use .... to give extra information about people.
> - We use .... to give extra information about things.
> - We use .... to give extra information about places.
> - We use .... to give extra information about possession.

(c) Join or rearrange the two sentences to make one. Use the word at the end. Take out the underlined words.

1 The films were made in New Zealand. The director Peter Jackson was born there. **(where)**

   The films were made in New Zealand, where the director Peter Jackson was born.

2 Elijah Wood became a big star after *The Lord of the Rings*. His career began when he was a child. **(whose)**

3 He had to stay away from home for 18 months. This was difficult for him. **(which)**

4 Tolkien couldn't find anyone to publish his books at first. He wrote the books in the 1950s. **(who)**

5 Frodo has to go to Sauron's kingdom. The final battle takes place there. **(where)**

3 Pronunciation

Pausing in non-defining relative clauses

🔊 Turn to page 121.

4 Grammar

Defining vs. non-defining relative clauses

> **Rule:**
> - In non-defining relative clauses the extra information is separated by commas.
>   *My brother, who is a doctor, lives in London.*
>   = I only have one brother. He lives in London and is a doctor.
> - In defining relative clauses we don't use commas.
>   *My brother who is a doctor lives in London.*
>   = I have more than one brother. One of them (the doctor) lives in London.

(a) Complete the sentences with *who, whose, that* or *where*. Check your answers in the text.

1 They are all fictional heroes .... adventures are filled with unbelievable danger.

2 It was fear .... gave Elijah Wood his chance.

3 It was a place .... Tolkien himself could feel safe.

4 Frodo is a hobbit .... speaks with a British accent.

(b) Defining or non-defining? Identify the non-defining relative clauses and put in the commas.

1 New Zealand where the films were made is a popular tourist destination.

2 It's the best film that I've ever seen.

3 Sally Campion whose brother wrote the story spent three years making the film.

4 That's the hotel where we always stay.

5 Speak

(a) Work with a partner. Match the titles and pictures of the films to the descriptions.

A A huge shark terrorises a sea resort. The local police chief tries to kill it.

B The crew of a spaceship find they have an unwelcome visitor on board.

C Three teenagers make a documentary about a legend in some woods.

D A writer takes a job looking after a hotel which has closed for the winter. Then the madness arrives.

(b) Work with a partner and discuss these questions.

1 Do you like scary films?

2 What's the most terrifying film you've ever seen? What made it so frightening?

3 Think of a horror film which you remember for its:

creepy music	special effects
blood and gore	monsters
sudden shocks	ghosts

1 *The Shining*

2 *Jaws*

3 *Alien*

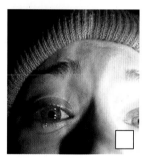

4 *The Blair Witch Project*

6 Listen

(a) 🔊 Listen to someone talking about *The Blair Witch Project*. Does the film use any of the items in the box in Exercise 5b to frighten its audiences?

(b) 🔊 Listen again and complete the summary. You should write one word or number in each space.

The Blair Witch Project was a big hit in ¹ .... It made more than ² .... at the box office. The film was cleverly advertised on the ³ .... by publishing rumours that said the film was ⁴ .... The story is about ⁵ .... film makers who make a ⁶ .... about the mythical Blair Witch, who lived in some ⁷ .... The film doesn't use the traditional techniques of horror films but plays on our own ⁸ .... to frighten its audience.

7 Vocabulary

Adjectives with prefixes

(a) Look at the example and put the adjectives in the correct columns to make their opposites.

comfortable	formal	patient	responsible
logical	possible	helpful	polite	regular
legal	expensive	~~afraid~~

un	im	in	ir	il
unafraid				

(b) Complete the sentences. Use an adjective with a prefix.

1 Do you talk while you're eating, or do you think it's very _impolite_ ?

2 Do you like to sleep on a hard bed or do you find it too .... ?

3 Do you use a dictionary when you do your English homework or do you find it .... ?

4 Are you good at waiting for things, or are you sometimes a little .... ?

5 If your parents went away for the weekend, would they leave you alone in the house or do they think you're too .... ?

6 How do you learn .... verbs in English?

(c) Work with a partner. Ask and answer the questions.

8 Grammar

Definite, indefinite and zero article

a Look at the examples. Match the examples with the rules.

a *Before it was released rumours appeared on **the** Internet.*

b ***The** film makers who made the film were never seen again.*

c *Horror films usually have creepy music.*

d *They made it using **a** video camera.*

e *~~Tolkien hated **the** attention caused by the success of his books.~~*

f *Tolkien was **a** professor in Oxford.*

g *She plays **the** piano really well.*

h *He's leaving hospital on Friday.*

Rule:

- We use *the* (definite article) to talk about:
  1 specific people, places, things ____*e*____
  2 if it's clear what we're talking about _____
  3 when there's only one of something _____
  4 musical instruments _____

- We use *a* or *an* (indefinite article) to talk about:
  5 one thing _____
  6 professions _____

- We don't use an article (zero article)
  7 to talk about people or things in general _____
  8 with *home, school, work, university, bed, hospital, church* and *prison* as institutions, not the buildings (especially after verbs *go to, get to, start, finish, leave, be in/at*)
  _____

b Complete the sentences with *the, a, an* or nothing.

1 I'd really like to be _____ archaeologist when I'm older.

2 Have you seen _____ moon tonight? It's beautiful.

3 I don't like _____ dogs.

4 Have you studied much for _____ test tomorrow?

5 He's bought _____ new computer.

6 Have you heard him play _____ guitar? He's fantastic.

7 He's still in _____ bed! It's almost midday.

8 I love _____ smell of spring.

c Look at the text. Some lines are correct and some have a word which should not be there. If a line is correct, put a tick (✓) in the space at the end of the line. If a word should not be there, cross it out and write the word in the space.

1	Last week Jasmine Smith, the most attractive girl at ~~the~~ school	*the*
2	agreed to go on a date with me. I decided to take her to the cinema	✓
3	to see a romantic comedy. I don't really like the romantic films	____
4	but I thought it would be perfect for a date. Unfortunately I left	____
5	the home late and when we got to the cinema there weren't any	____
6	tickets left. The only film which still had the tickets was a horror	____
7	film. I couldn't believe it. My romantic date was ruined. To my	____
8	surprise Jasmine suggested seeing the horror film so we bought	____
9	tickets and went in. What a great decision! I was so scared that I	____
10	spent the whole film holding Jasmine's hand. Jasmine thought I was	____
11	cute. She says she likes the men who don't pretend to be brave.	____

Fiction in mind

9 Read

a Part of the story is set in Inishbofin, a small island off the west coast of Ireland. What do you think life on the island is like? Think of the people, the climate and the landscape.

The Lady in White

by Colin Campbell

The story

John is a successful TV producer with a happy family life. He wants to make a programme about the strange story of a hitch-hiker. Then he finds out that the story and the things that have happened in his own life are very similar. He begins to worry about his wife and young child and that he may be going mad ...

But as he woke now, he did not feel comfortable. He did not like the darkness of the room where he lay. It made him feel nervous. He felt something was not quite right. Slowly, from the
5 darkness, he began to recognise shapes: the lighter-coloured walls and the dark shapes of the heavy furniture in the cottage – the large wardrobe at the end of the bed where they put their clothes and where they could have put twice as many clothes, the painting on the wall of
10 the two men on the beach pushing their little boat into the high waves of the Atlantic.

As he began to realise where he was he also knew that something was very wrong. The room was quiet. Quieter than it should be. He could hear only the
15 outside noises of the sea and a wind that whispered through the windows of the cottage. There were no noises from inside the cottage. He reached over in the bed towards Rachel, but knew already before his hand touched the cold sheets that she was not there. He sat up
20 in bed and tried to say her name but nothing came out. He tried to shout but nothing came. His breathing was fast and very loud. He pulled the sheets back and threw them off the bed and saw that it was still empty. He got out of bed and ran to the wardrobe and opened it and
25 looked inside it. Then he ran to the window and pulled back the curtains. He looked out into the darkness, pushing his face against the cold wet window and silently called Rachel's name. He could see no-one outside. He turned to the little bed where Patrick lay and tried to scream again as he saw that the bed was 30 empty too.

He ran to the living room, pushing and kicking at the furniture that got in his way. He screamed her name and this time it came out; from the bottom of his stomach the name came and he put his hands to his ears 35 to stop it. It hurt so much to hear her name when she was not there, when she had gone.

He ran to the front door and pulled at it but it did not move. The key was in the lock and he turned it. But it simply turned and turned and the lock did not move. 40 He ran back to the bedroom and stopped suddenly as he saw that the wardrobe door was opening. It opened slowly and someone stepped out. It was someone in black. The white of the face was the only light in the room. It was impossible to see if it was a man or a 45 woman. It was carrying something. It spoke. The voice was the man's from the boat.

'The baby's fine. Don't worry.' And John saw that the man was holding Patrick.

b 🔊 Read, listen and answer the questions.

1. What time of day was it?
2. What did the painting on the wall show?
3. Why did he know there was something wrong?
4. What did he try and do when he found that Rachel was missing?
5. What did he do in the living room?
6. What happened after he ran back into the bedroom?

Discussion box

Work in pairs or small groups. Discuss these questions together.

1. Who do you think the man from the boat is?
2. Who is Patrick? What do you think happened to him?
3. Do you believe in ghosts?
4. Have you ever experienced something you couldn't explain?
5. Do you know any ghost stories?

10 Vocabulary

Phrasal verbs with *sit*

(a) Look at the sentence from the story.

*He **sat up** in bed and tried to say her name ...*

Here are some other phrasal verbs with *sit*. Match them with their definitions.

1 sit out   a to listen to or watch something that is long and boring
2 sit through   b to be a model for an artist or photographer
3 sit for   c to wait for something to happen without making any effort
4 sit back   d to be unable to take part in an activity, often because of an injury

(b) Complete the sentences with the appropriate phrasal verbs.

1 The Queen was asked to .... the famous painter Lucian Freud.
2 Rooney .... the football game because of a broken ankle.
3 You can't just .... and wait for money to come to you!
4 We had to .... two hours of speeches before we got dinner.

11 Write

(a) Read the film review. Does the writer like the film?

(b) Read the review again and answer the questions.

1 Which paragraph contains:
   a a recommendation?
   b the storyline?
   c an analysis?

2 Why doesn't the writer tell the whole story?

3 What does the writer like about the film?

(c) Write a review of a film you really like. Use the review on *Psycho* to help you. Write 120–180 words.

One of the scariest films I've ever seen is *Psycho*. It was made in 1960 by the master of suspense, Alfred Hitchcock. The story is about a young woman called Marion Crane who, one Friday afternoon, is asked by her employer to deposit $40,000 in the bank. Marion is tempted by the money and decides to drive off with it. However, halfway on her journey she starts to feel guilty and decides to turn back and return the money. Because it is dark and raining she stops for the night at the Bates Motel, which is run by shy and sensitive Norman Bates.

Despite being more than 40 years old, *Psycho* continues to frighten modern audiences. The story is fantastic and keeps you guessing until the end. Hitchcock doesn't use special effects or lots of blood and gore to scare the audience, but prefers to use unusual camera angles and creepy music to create the atmosphere. It isn't full of sudden shocks but when they come they really do make you jump – the famous shower scene is a perfect example of this. Finally, Anthony Perkins gives a great performance as Norman Bates.

Don't be put off because it's an old film or because it's in black and white – *Psycho* is a fantastic film and really one of the all-time cinema classics.

For your portfolio

16 Happiness

✱ *be used to doing something* vs. *used to do*
✱ Grammar of phrasal verbs
✱ Vocabulary: expressions with *feel*
✱ Vocabulary: expressions with prepositions

the weather

how much money you have

the thing(s) you are doing

the people you are with

1 Read and listen

a Look at the pictures. Which of these things affect how happy or unhappy you are?

b Read the article and answer the questions.

1 When and why did the professor start thinking about happiness?
2 What is 'flow'?

The 'Flow' of Happiness

A lot of people in the world today are used to working, going on holiday, and having money – but many of them aren't happy. Yet other people seem to be really happy, even if they are poor, or have no job, or are surrounded by problems. Why?

Professor Mihaly Csikszentmihalyi, from the University of Chicago, has interviewed thousands of people who have a happy life to find out how they do it. 'I've been studying happiness for over 30 years,' says Csikszentmihalyi. 'My interest in the subject came from my own experience as a child during World War II, when I saw many adults destroyed by the terrible events. But there were always a few who kept their courage, helped others, and were able to give a sense of purpose and meaning to their lives. I wanted to find out how a person could build a fulfilling and enjoyable life.'

In general, his research showed that people were unhappy doing nothing. The professor stresses that happy people don't waste time, either at work or when they're free. 'Many people feel that the time they spend at work or at school is wasted. But often their *free* time is also wasted. Many people are used to doing passive things – watching television, for example – without using any skills. As a result, life goes past in a series of boring experiences.'

But it doesn't have to be this way. The professor has found that people are happy when they get into something he calls 'flow'. When people get very involved in a task that they have chosen, and which is well-defined and challenging, they experience 'flow', a state where they don't notice time passing.

They also experience enjoyment. Professor Csikszentmihalyi makes a contrast between enjoyment and pleasure. 'I used to think they were the same thing – but they're not! Pleasure is a big bowl of ice cream, or taking a hot bath on a cold day – nothing bad at all! But enjoyment is about doing something and achieving something. It isn't really important *what* we do, it's more important to *do something*, and feel positive about it, and to try to do it well.'

People who are not used to happiness can learn how to be happy, says the professor, if they constantly get into 'flow' states. Is happiness as easy as that? Perhaps it is.

Discussion box

Work in pairs or small groups. Discuss these questions together.

1 Can you think of other passive activities?
2 What things do you do to create 'flow'?

c 🔊 Read the text again and listen. Mark the statements *T* (true) or *F* (false). Correct the false statements.

1 Csikszentmihalyi has been studying happiness for more than 30 years. ☐

2 Csikszentmihalyi thinks that many people use their free time well. ☐

3 He thinks that watching TV is a passive thing. ☐

4 We can experience 'flow' when we do things that are impossible for us. ☐

5 People in 'flow' can easily forget what time it is. ☐

6 Enjoyment and pleasure are the same thing. ☐

2 Grammar

be used to (doing) something

a Complete the sentences. Use the text to check your ideas.

1 Many people are used to .... passive things.

2 People who are not used to .... can learn how to be happy.

b We use *be used to (doing) something* to talk about experience and habits.

I'm really tired. I'm not used to getting up so early.
(I find it difficult because I usually get up later.)

I didn't understand him at first but now I'm used to his accent.
(With experience I find it easier.)

c Look at the examples in Exercises 2a and 2b and (circle) the correct words.

> **Rule:**
> • *be used to* is followed by a noun / an adjective or by an infinitive / a gerund.

d Irene is Spanish. She is living in London. Use the words in the box to complete her sentences.

> working   British money   sunshine
> going   ~~driving~~   weather   speaking
> laughing   ~~traffic~~   having

1 I'm from Madrid, so I'm used to the heavy ...*traffic*... , but I'm still not used to ...*driving*... on the left!

2 I'm not really used to the .... yet – it rains so much here. In Madrid I was used to .... almost everyday.

3 I'm not used to .... from 9am to 5pm every day. In Madrid I was used to .... a siesta after lunch.

4 I'm already used to using .... But the shops here close at 5.30. I'm not used to .... home so early.

5 I had some British friends in Madrid so I was already used to .... English before I arrived.

6 British humour is difficult. I think I'm used to .... at different kinds of things.

3 Grammar

be used to doing vs. *used to do*

a Remember that *used to (do)* is a way of talking about habits or situations in the past that are not true any more:

We used to go out every weekend. (= but now we don't)

I didn't use to drive but now I go everywhere by car. (= I drive now)

This is different from *be used to (doing)*:

I used to live in London, but now I live in Paris and I'm used to speaking French every day.

b Complete the sentences. Use the correct form of *be used to* or *used to*.

1 I ...*used to hate*.. (hate) vegetables but now I love them.

2 We live next to a busy road so I .... (sleep) with lots of noise.

3 He's a bit nervous because he .... (not speak) in public.

4 She .... (not like) children but now she's got four of her own.

5 I'm exhausted. I .... (not walk) so far.

6 We .... (live) in the city but we moved to the country last year.

7 I didn't recognise you. You .... (not wear) glasses, did you?

8 I've worked in Argentina for five years so I .... (speak) Spanish.

4 Listen

a) Look at the pictures. Guess what *happiness* means for the people in the pictures.

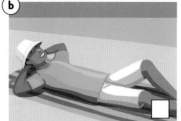

b) 🔊 Two students from a British school are doing a survey about happiness. Listen to their interviews. Number the pictures in the order that you hear them. Write 1–6 in the boxes.

c) 🔊 Listen again and complete what the people said about happiness.

1 Happiness comes from inside you. You can be happy .... you are.

2 Being with my .... and my .... – that's happiness!

3 And then the plane .... off, and it's that moment, that .... of freedom.

4 What I do is .... for other people. And most of my passengers are really thankful.

5 I'd love to live in a warm .... , you know, where you can get a nice ....

6 I eat it very slowly, ... by .... And I feel great!

5 Speak

Work with a partner and discuss these questions.

1 Which of the things in the interviews about happiness do you agree/disagree with?

2 Has your idea of happiness changed since you were a small child? What used to make you happy that is not important for you any more? What makes you happy now that wasn't important for you then?

6 Vocabulary

feel

a) Look at the last interview in Exercise 4c. How does the woman feel?

b) Here are some words that are often used with the verb *feel*. Complete the sentences with the words in the box.

> ~~fine~~   confident   the need   sorry for
> lonely   stupid   strange   up to

1 I was ill last weekend, but I feel ......*fine*...... again now.

2 I went back to my primary school after ten years, and it felt really .... to be there again.

3 Jane's grandmother died last week. I feel really .... her.

4 No, I don't want to go out tonight – I'm tired and I don't feel .... it.

5 I've studied really hard for the exams, and I feel .... I'm going to do well.

6 I don't know why you feel .... to criticise people all the time!

7 I didn't make any friends in China and, to be honest, I felt very ....

8 I met Pete Smith in town yesterday – but I couldn't remember his name! I felt really ....

7 Grammar
Phrasal verbs

(a) Many phrasal verbs have two parts. <u>Underline</u> the two parts of each phrasal verb in these sentences.

1 I bumped into an old friend the other day.
2 My dad's car broke down yesterday.
3 We sorted the problem out.
4 I looked the word up in my dictionary.

(b) Compare sentences 1 and 2 in Exercise 7a with sentences 3 and 4. What do you notice about the two parts of each phrasal verb?

Rule:

- With some phrasal verbs, the two parts cannot be separated. They have to be together.
  *I **bumped into** an old friend.* Not: ~~I bumped an old friend into~~.

- Other phrasal verbs can be separated, and we can put an object between the two parts.
  *We **sorted** the problem **out**.*
  *We **sorted out** the problem.*

- When we use a pronoun (*him, it, them*, etc.) with phrasal verbs that can be separated, we must put it between the two parts of the verb.
  *We **sorted** it **out**.* Not: ~~We sorted out it~~.

Look

How do you know if a phrasal verb can be separated or not? Use a dictionary to find out!

> **look sb/sth up** to look at a book or computer in order to find information *I looked it up in the dictionary.*

If the word *somebody* or *something* is in the middle of the verb this phrasal verb **can be separated**.

> **look after sb/sth** to take care of someone or something by keeping them healthy or in a good condition *Could you look after the children while I'm out?*

If the word *somebody* or *something* is at the end, this phrasal verb **cannot be separated**.

Some phrasal verbs have three or more parts. These cannot usually be split.
*I **look up to** my dad.* Or *I **look up to** him.*
*I **get on well with** my sister.* Or *I **get on well with** her.*

(c) Put the words in the correct order to make sentences. Sometimes there is more than one possibility.

1 story / made / you / up / that
   You made that story up.
   or
   You made up that story.

2 he / father / after / his / takes

3 put / they / us / up / tonight / can't

4 Italian / up / I / on / holiday / in / picked / Italy

5 up / you / with / how / put / noise / do / that

8 Pronunciation
Stress in phrasal verbs

🔊 Turn to page 121.

9 Speak and listen

a What makes your day good? What makes your day bad? Work with a partner. Student B: Turn to page 122. Student A: Ask your partner these questions and answer their questions. You start.

b How do these things make you feel? Write ☹ (in a bad mood) or 😐 (doesn't bother me).

1 You make a hot drink and forget to drink it.
2 It rains all day.
3 Your mum or dad asks you to go shopping for them.
4 You've got a headache.
5 You miss the bus into town.
6 You're late for school.
7 You get soaked in the rain.
8 You can't get to sleep.

c 🔊 Listen to the song and tick the things in Exercise 9b that happen to the singer.

d 🔊 Listen again and complete the sentences.

> **On a good day ...**
> What time do you get out of bed?
> Something happens in the morning. What is it?
> What do you have for lunch?
> Someone calls you. Who is it?
> How do you spend the evening?
> What time do you get to bed?

Thank You
by Dido

My [1]_____'s gone cold, I'm wondering why I got out of bed at all
The morning rain clouds up my [2]_____ and I can't see at all
And even if I could it'd all be grey, but your [3]_____ on my wall
It reminds me that it's not so bad, it's not so bad

I drank too much last night, got [4]_____ to pay,
    my head just feels in pain
I missed the [5]_____ and there'll be hell today,
    I'm late for work again
And even if I'm there, they'll all imply that I might not last
    the [6]_____
And then you call me and it's not so bad, it's not so bad and ...

I want to thank you for giving me the best day of my life
Oh, just to be with you is having the best day of my life

Push the door, I'm [7]_____ at last and I'm soaking through
    and through
Then you handed me a [8]_____ and all I see is you
And even if my house falls [9]_____ now, I wouldn't have a clue
Because you're near me and ...

> **Did you know ...?**
> British songwriter and singer Dido (real name Florian Cloud de Bounevialle Armstrong) had more early success in the USA than her homeland. But when top rap star Eminem used *Thank You* as a sample on his hit single *Stan*, Dido suddenly found herself famous all over the world.

(e) Discuss the questions with a partner.

1 What kind of day is the singer having? Why?

2 Why does she say she's having the best day of her life?

3 How does her partner make her feel happy?

4 Who are the people in your life who make you feel happy? How do they do it?

10 Vocabulary

Expressions with prepositions

(a) In the song the singer says she's *soaked through and through*. What do you think *through and through* means?

(b) Here are some more expressions with two prepositions. Decide with a partner what you think they mean.

1 He was ill in bed for two months but he's <u>up and about</u> now.

2 Things have been <u>up and down</u> for me recently but hopefully they'll get better soon.

3 She's <u>on the up and up</u>. I think she's going to be really famous soon.

4 My dad is so boring. He just goes <u>on and on</u> about why I should study harder.

5 She's not very well. She's been <u>in and out</u> of hospital all year.

(c) Use the expressions to complete the sentences.

1 There's no need to go _____ about it. I've said I'm sorry.

2 He's a bank manager now but when he was younger he was _____ of prison all the time.

3 I hear Dana's been ill in bed for a while. Do you know when she'll be _____ again?

4 We're doing quite well. Business seems to be _____ .

5 His school work's a bit _____ . He needs to concentrate more.

11 Write

(a) Complete the poem with the words in the box.

Always Perfect Icy ~~Having~~ Staying
Sleeping Parties Never Eating

1 _Having_ fun with friends
2 _____ feeling free
3 _____ every weekend
4 _____ grades at school
5 _____ winter mornings
6 _____ –ending sun
7 _____ whatever I want to
8 _____ up all night
9 _____ until midday

(b) Take the first letter of each line and read downwards. What word does it spell out?

(c) Write your own poem, using the letters of *A Perfect Day.*

For your portfolio

1 Grammar

a Complete the sentences and questions. Use the correct form of reported speech.

1 'I like the present,' Jim said.
   Jim said that _he liked the present._

2 'Are you hungry?'
   Mum asked ....

3 'We'll come to your party,' my friends said.
   My friends said ....

4 'Where is the hotel?'
   Kim asked ....

5 'I lived in Paris for three years,' Zoe said.
   Zoe said ....

6 'Can I help you?'
   Nick asked ....

7 'I must leave at 7 o'clock,' Maria said.
   Maria said ....

8 'What's your favourite film?'
   Pete asked ....

9 'How old are you?'
   Alicia asked ....

[8]

b Circle the correct words.

1 My friend *said / told* me to meet him at the station.

2 We *apologised / suggested* for being late.

3 The doctor *said / told* me to stay in bed.

4 He *invited / offered* to drive us home.

5 They *asked / refused* him to help.

6 Our teacher *explained / told* how we should do it.

7 I *invited / suggested* going for a coffee.

8 Mark has *invited / offered* me to his party on Friday.

9 Frances *apologised / refused* to take any money for the book.

10 She *begged / offered* me to forgive her.

[9]

c Write a sentence with *if*.

1 I didn't see you. I didn't say hello.
   If I'd seen you, I would have said hello.

2 I didn't finish my homework because I didn't have time.
   ....

3 I bought the motorbike because Ben gave me the money.
   ....

4 I didn't go to see the film because I had seen it before.
   ....

5 We arrived at the restaurant late, so we didn't get a table.
   ....

6 I didn't get taxi because I didn't have enough money.
   ....

7 I got up late and I missed the bus.
   ....

[6]

d Read the information and complete the sentences. Use a relative clause. Sometimes the clause tells you which thing or person (defining) and sometimes it gives you extra information (non-defining). Use commas where necessary.

1 There is a woman living next door. She is a doctor.
   The woman _who lives next door is a doctor_ .

2 Hip-hop music started in the USA, and its popularity is increasing.
   The popularity of hip-hop music ....

3 We met some people. Their car had broken down.
   We met some people ....

4 Ron is spending his next holiday in Florida. He was born there.
   Ron is spending ....

5 Kate works in a café. The café sells Italian food.
   Kate works ....

6 Mrs Norris is going on holiday to Spain. Her family live there.
   Mrs Norris is going ....

[5]

e Complete the sentences with *the*, *a*, *an* or nothing.

1 For me, London is _the_ most attractive city in the world.

2 Can you show me .... email that John wrote?

3 Helen is .... engineer and her brother is .... teacher.

4 .... girls usually spend more money on clothes than .... boys.

5 Patrick's going to .... university next year.

6 Charlotte plays .... flute and Annie plays .... piano.

[8]

f Complete the sentences. Use the correct form of *used to* or *be used to*.

1 She works in a hospital. She _is used to dealing_ (deal) with a lot of stress.
2 I _____ (not do) a lot of sport but now I run half an hour every day.
3 We _____ (not stay up) so late. We want to go to bed now.
4 She _____ (send) 50 text messages a day. She doesn't do that any more.
5 I live in Rome, so I _____ (drive) in a big city.
6 He _____ (play) a lot of football but he has given it up.
7 He speaks very good French. _____ he _____ (live) in France?
8 I do a paper round every morning so I _____ (get up) early. **[7]**

g (Circle) the correct order in each sentence. Sometimes there is more than one possibility.

1 Sorry I'm late, but I *bumped John into /* (bumped into John) on the way home.
2 I think she *takes her father after / takes after her father*. They're both hot-headed!
3 I'm not sure if I can *pick you up / pick up you* tomorrow.
4 My Dad's great! I really *look up to him / look him up to*.
5 We want to visit Cambridge. Could you *put up us / put us up* for a week?
6 I have to *look my little brother after / look after my little brother* on Saturday mornings.
7 Don't worry I've *sorted out the problem / sorted the problem out*. **[6]**

2 Vocabulary

a Complete the sentences with the words in the box.

> independent determined bad-tempered
> ambitious imaginative

1 Mark is so _____ . Nobody can stop him doing something.
2 Everybody says I'm _____ and it's true that I want to be very successful.
3 She argues with everyone – she's so _____ !
4 Science fiction writing is the perfect job for Jon. He was always very _____ as a teenager.
5 He never needs any help. He's very _____ . **[5]**

b Write the correct word in each space.

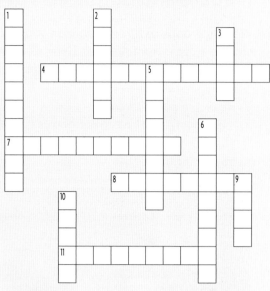

Across

4 A line in the middle of someone's hair, made by brushing it in two different directions (2 words).
7 Bits of hair which are lighter than the natural colour.
8 Small lines in the skin, caused by old age.
11 Hair which a man grows above his mouth.

Down

1 A layer of fat between the face and neck (2 words).
2 A permanent picture or word on the skin.
3 Attractively thin.
5 A hairstyle in which the hair is tied up high at the back of the head and hangs down as on a horse.
6 The short hairs which grow along the edges of the eye.
9 A mark left on part of the body after an injury or a cut has healed.
10 A polite word for fat. **[11]**

How did you do?

Tick (✓) a box for each section.

Total score:	🙂	😐	🙁
65	Very good	OK	Not very good
Grammar	37 – 49	25 – 36	less than 25
Vocabulary	13 – 16	8 – 12	less than 8

Project 1
A class survey: who we are

1 Prepare and do the survey

(a) Work in groups of three or four. In your group, choose a topic from the box. Think of four or five questions you can ask other students.

> Free time activities
> Technology we have in our homes
> Earning money
> Spending money

(b) Make a questionnaire with your questions. Here are some possibilities:

> 1 Give a number to each of these activities from 1–10 (1 is most boring and 10 is most interesting):
>   visiting relatives ☐
>   playing a computer game with somebody ☐

> 1 How much time do you spend on the Internet each week?
> 2 How many DVD players / video recorders are there in your house?

> 1 How do you earn money?
>   Saturday job ....
>   Babysitting ....

> 1 How much per month do you spend on each of these things?
>   sweets, chocolate, etc. ....
>   clothes ....

(c) Use your questionnaire. Ask the other students in your class and note their answers. Make sure everyone has answered.

2 Write up the results

(a) Go back to your group and put all your answers together. What conclusions can you reach from your results?

(b) Use the information to prepare a report on your group's topic. Organise your information into paragraphs. For some information you could also draw a chart. See page 11 for an example of a report.

How much per month do you spend on each of these things?

3 Present your report

Present your report to the class. Each person should present one part.

Project 2

A group presentation

1 The situation

Work in groups of three or four. Your group was travelling in a small plane which crashed on an island in the Pacific Ocean. You are the only survivors, and the plane was destroyed. You have looked around the island and there are no buildings, no people, no animals, but there is a river, a lot of fruit and a lot of insects.

2 To help you survive

In your group, choose any six (but only six!) of these things. Think about why you want them and what you will use them for:

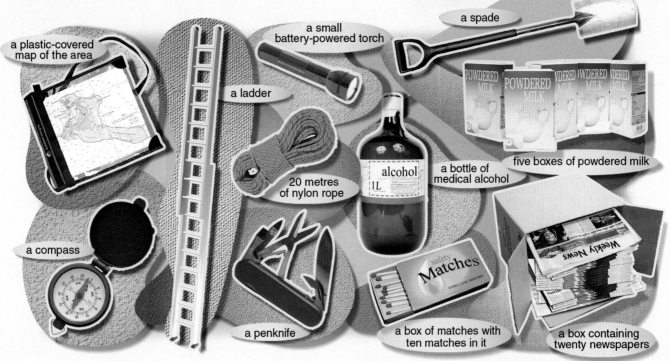

a plastic-covered map of the area

a small battery-powered torch

a spade

a ladder

five boxes of powdered milk

20 metres of nylon rope

a bottle of medical alcohol

a compass

a penknife

a box of matches with ten matches in it

a box containing twenty newspapers

3 Prepare the presentation

After three months on the island you are home again! A British company wants to make a TV programme about your experiences, but needs more information. In your group, look at the questions and prepare your answers:

- What were the six things that you had with you?
- How did you use them to help you survive or escape?
- What did you eat and drink?
- How did you feel when you were on the island?
- Were there any especially difficult moments while you were on the island?
- How did you manage to get off the island – did your group do it alone, or did other people help you?
- How do you feel now?

4 Presentation

(a) Decide who is going to talk about which answer. Everyone in the group should say something.

(b) Rehearse your presentation.

(c) Groups take turns to give their presentation to the rest of the class.

For your portfolio

Project 3
A poster: a mystery

aliens

The Loch Ness monster

crop circles

Stonehenge

ghosts

1 Do your research

a Work with a partner. Choose a mystery. This could be something well known, as in the pictures above, or perhaps something local.

b Research some information to find out as much as you can about your mystery. Use the Internet, your school library and magazines and books.

2 Make the poster

a Find some pictures of your mystery for your poster – download from the Internet, cut out from magazines or draw some.

b Use the information you found to write two texts about your mystery. Include:

some background about the mystery

- a description of the mystery and where it is
- some history (e.g. who first discovered it and when?)
- its importance today, e.g. is it a big tourist attraction?

some theories about the mystery

- common opinion today
- any other less popular theories
- any local theories or legends
- what you believe

c Do a class survey. Think of an interesting question about your mystery and ask as many students as possible for their opinion.

What do you think Stonehenge was?

Do you believe the US government knows more about UFOs than it tells us?

d At the top of a large piece of paper, write the title of your presentation and arrange your pictures and texts on the poster.

e At the bottom of the paper, write a text about your class's opinions. Use the information you found in Exercise 2c to make a pie-chart to put on your poster.

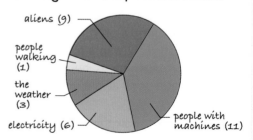

How do you think crop circles are made?

aliens (9)

people walking (1)

the weather (3)

electricity (6)

people with machines (11)

3 Presentation

Present your poster to the class. Be prepared to answer questions about it.

For your portfolio

Project 4
Designing a website

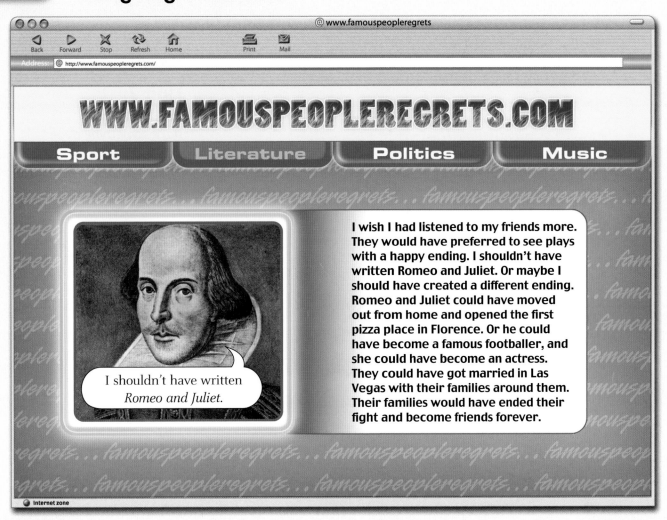

1 Prepare your website

a) Work in groups of three or four. You are going to create a humorous website on the regrets of famous people.

b) Look at the web page above. What links are there? Which famous people do you think are on the different links?

c) In your group, think of famous people you want on your website. Think of one famous person for each link. Write a list.

d) Discuss what each of the famous people in your list achieved / have achieved. Make notes. Think of funny ideas why the famous people might have regretted the things they did.

2 Make your website

a) Each student in your group chooses a famous person from your list and writes a text.

b) When all the texts are finished, work together on the language in each text. Read through all the texts in your group and make notes on what could be improved. Discuss the suggestions and rewrite the texts.

c) Find some pictures that relate to your text from magazines, books or the Internet. Put all the texts and the pictures on a large piece of paper. Arrange them so that the other students can see which text belongs to which link.

d) When all the groups have finished, put your web pages somewhere where everyone can see them. Compare what different groups have done.

For your portfolio

Pronunciation exercises

Unit 1

Schwa /ə/ in prepositions and articles

a) 🔊 Listen to the sentences. How do you pronounce the <u>underlined</u> words?

1 <u>The</u> majority <u>of</u> girls prefer music <u>to</u> sport.
2 Over half <u>of</u> us think shopping is better <u>than</u> school.
3 Less <u>than</u> a third <u>of</u> our class prefer books <u>to</u> films.
4 Girls tend <u>to</u> spend £2 <u>a</u> week more <u>than</u> boys.
5 It is quite common <u>for</u> 10–16-year-olds <u>to</u> have some kind <u>of</u> job.

b) 🔊 Listen again and repeat.

Unit 2

Sentence stress: rhythm in questions

a) 🔊 Listen to the questions and mark the stressed words.

1 Can you tell us another secret?
2 Was it really that easy?
3 So how can I use it?
4 What on earth is that?
5 What can I do to communicate better?

b) 🔊 Listen again and repeat.

Unit 3

Linking sounds

a) 🔊 Listen to the sentences. How do you pronounce the <u>underlined</u> parts?

1 I always <u>stick up</u> for my friends.
2 I can't lie, but I don't want to <u>tell on</u> a friend.
3 That's a good reason <u>to fall out</u>.
4 I'm <u>surprised anyone gets on</u> with you.

b) 🔊 Listen again and repeat.

Unit 4

/ɔː/ short

a) 🔊 Listen and repeat.

1 more   2 four   3 before
4 saw   5 short   6 bought
7 caught   8 court   9 ought
10 forty

b) 🔊 <u>Underline</u> the syllables with the /ɔː/ sound. Then listen, check and repeat.

1 I saw the ball, and I caught it.
2 We can't play tennis here – the court's too short!
3 We ought to buy four more.
4 But we bought forty before!

Unit 5

/gənə/ going to

a) 🔊 Listen to the sentences. How do you pronounce the <u>underlined</u> parts?

1 Hurry up – we're <u>going to</u> be late!
2 She's <u>going to</u> sail round the world.
3 I think I'm <u>going to</u> sneeze.
4 He isn't <u>going to</u> come.
5 Do you think it's <u>going to</u> rain?

b) 🔊 Listen again and repeat.

Unit 6

Weak and strong forms of prepositions

a) 🔊 Listen to the sentences. Circle the prepositions where they are weak. <u>Underline</u> the prepositions where they are strong.

1 I'm revising for my exams.
2 What are you looking for?
3 I can't stand talking to him.
4 Who's John talking to?
5 Who are you looking at?
6 I think he's at work.
7 You can leave if you want to.
8 We're going to London for the weekend.

b) 🔊 Which sentences put a stronger stress on the preposition? Why? Listen, check and repeat.

Unit 7

Stress pattern in *have something done*

a) 🔊 Listen and mark the words that are stressed.

1 Have you had your hair cut?
2 Dad's going to have a phone installed.
3 They had the road closed.
4 They had the people removed.
5 Have you had your camera fixed?
6 He's having a garage built.

b) 🔊 Listen again and repeat.

Unit 8

/aʊ/ allowed

a) 🔊 Listen and repeat.

1 cow   2 house   3 round
4 town   5 shower   6 allowed

b) 🔊 <u>Underline</u> the syllables with the /aʊ/ sound. Then listen, check and repeat.

1 How are you now?
2 I'm allowed to have a mouse in the house.
3 You aren't allowed to sing loudly in the shower.
4 We're allowed to walk the cow around the town.

Unit 9

Stress in nouns, adjectives and verbs

a) 🔊 <u>Underline</u> the syllables you think are stressed. Then listen and check.

1 imagine   2 imagination
3 refer   4 reference   5 popular
6 popularity   7 possible
8 possibility   9 relax
10 relaxation

b) 🔊 Listen again and repeat.

Unit 10

I wish ... and if only ...

a 🔊 Listen to the sentences. How do you pronounce the <u>underlined</u> parts?

1 <u>If only</u> there was something to do.
2 <u>If only</u> she liked me.
3 <u>If only</u> they'd ask me.
4 <u>If only</u> he knew.
5 <u>I wish I</u> knew his name.
6 <u>I wish I</u> could go home.
7 <u>I wish you</u> weren't so noisy.

b 🔊 Listen again and repeat.

Unit 11

/əʊ/ though

a 🔊 Listen and repeat.

1 so   2 go   3 don't
4 slow   5 nobody   6 though
7 although   8 won't

b 🔊 <u>Underline</u> the syllables with the /əʊ/ sound. Then listen, check and repeat.

1 Don't go so slowly.
2 I won't watch the game show.
3 Although I know Alex, I don't know his brother.
4 Nobody likes him, even though he's friendly.

Unit 12

have in must have / might have / can't have / couldn't have

a 🔊 Listen to the sentences. Circle the examples of *have* where it is weak. <u>Underline</u> the examples of *have* when it is stressed.

1 She must have been very happy.
2 Yes, she must have. She was smiling a lot.
3 I might have passed the exam.
4 You can't have. You didn't study.
5 They must have walked here.
6 Well, they can't have come by car – they haven't got one!
7 Oh no! I can't have lost my keys again!
8 You must have left them in the car.

9 He couldn't have known the answers.
10 He must have. He passed the test.

b 🔊 Which sentences put a stronger stress on *have*? Why? Listen, check and repeat.

Unit 13

Intonation in reported questions

a 🔊 Listen to the sentences. Does the speaker's voice go up or down at the end? Write ↑ (up) or ↓ (down).

1 Have you got a girlfriend?
2 He asked me if I had a girlfriend.
3 Did you finish the homework?
4 She asked me if I had finished the homework.
5 Do you live near here?
6 He asked me if I lived near here.
7 Are you enjoying the party?
8 He asked me if I was enjoying the party.
9 Do you want a cup of tea?
10 She asked if I wanted a cup of tea.

b 🔊 Listen again and repeat.

Unit 14

should have / shouldn't have

a 🔊 Listen to the sentences. How do you pronounce the <u>underlined</u> parts?

1 I'm sorry – I <u>shouldn't have</u> done that.
2 He <u>should have</u> left earlier.
3 You <u>shouldn't have</u> forgotten her birthday.
4 They <u>shouldn't have</u> driven so fast.
5 Your brother <u>shouldn't have</u> hit me.
6 I <u>should have</u> asked more questions.

b 🔊 Listen again and repeat.

Unit 15

Pausing in non-defining relative clauses

When there is a non-defining relative clause in the middle of a sentence, we usually pause at the beginning and at the end of the relative clause to add the extra information. The voice also goes down a little.

a 🔊 Listen to the sentences. Write commas where the voice pauses.

1 Peter Jackson who was born in New Zealand directed *The Lord of the Rings*.
2 J.R.R. Tolkien who was a very shy man wrote many books.
3 My sister who lives in Hong Kong writes stories for children.
4 Manchester which is in the north of England gets a lot of rain every year.
5 My best friend whose father is a doctor wants to study medicine at university.
6 Elijah Wood whose career began when he was a child became a big star after *The Lord of the Rings*.

b 🔊 Listen again and repeat.

Unit 16

Stress in phrasal verbs

a 🔊 Listen to the sentences. Circle the prepositions that are weak. <u>Underline</u> the prepositions that are stressed.

1 You made that story up.
2 Did you just make up that story?
3 We can work the problem out.
4 We can work out the problem.
5 Please take off your shoes when you arrive.
6 Take your jacket off and have a cup of tea.
7 I looked up my old friends on the Internet.
8 I looked it up in the dictionary.

b 🔊 Which sentences put a stronger stress on the preposition? Why? Listen again and repeat.

Speaking exercises: extra material

Unit 2, page 15, Exercise 9

Student B: Complete the questions with *say* or *tell*. Then ask your partner the questions. Student A starts.

1 Can you .... your name backwards?
2 Have you ever .... something out loud at the wrong time?
3 Can you .... me a secret?
4 Do your parents always know when you're not .... the truth?
5 When was the last time your parents .... you off, and what was it for?

Unit 9, page 65, Exercise 8

Student B: Write your answers to these things on a piece of paper.

- something you started to do but gave up.
- something you remember doing when you were ten years old.
- something you stopped doing when you became a teenager.
- something you love doing.

Look at your partner's answers and guess what they refer to. Student A starts.

walking to school

A: *Is that something you love doing?*
B: *No, that's something I started doing when I became a teenager.*

Unit 11, page 74, Exercise 1

Student B: Read text B and answer the questions.

1 How did the film crew change the beach?
2 What was the result of planting coconut trees?
3 What did they do to make the sand stay on the beach? Did it work?
4 Did it rain more than normal?
5 Did the film crew pay a lot of money to the local people?
6 What did tourists think of the island when they visited it after the film was made?

Text B

When the film crew decided to use our island, we thought it would be very good for us, good for tourism – this is important because most people can only make money from fishing. And, of course, maybe we would get to meet Leonardo DiCaprio!

The trouble started when they wanted to change the beach. They brought in big machines, bulldozers, to take away the natural vegetation and make the sand level so they that they could film more easily, and they put in some coconut trees to make it look 'more beautiful'. However, these trees were not native to our island, and they killed other plant life. This made the sand weak. They put some wooden poles in the sand to stop it moving, but in spite of this protection the normal monsoon rain washed the sand into the sea. This is a problem you can't just ignore. You see, all that sand damaged the coral reefs, and that's where we fish. So we couldn't fish anymore.

Even though they gave us money, it wasn't enough to really help us. Of course, a lot of tourists came to see where *The Beach* was filmed, but they were shocked when they saw how bad it looked.

Unit 16, page 112, Exercise 9

Student B: Ask your partner these questions and answer their questions. Student A starts.

On a bad day ...

What time do you get out of bed?
Something happens in the morning. What is it?
What do you have for lunch?
Someone calls you. Who is it?
How do you spend the evening?
What time do you get to bed?

Irregular verbs and phonetics

Irregular verbs

Base form	Past simple	Past participle
be	was/were	been
become	became	become
begin	began	begun
blow	blew	blown
break	broke	broken
bring	brought	brought
build	built	built
buy	bought	bought
can	could	been able
catch	caught	caught
choose	chose	chosen
come	came	come
cost	cost	cost
cut	cut	cut
do	did	done
drink	drank	drunk
drive	drove	driven
eat	ate	eaten
fall	fell	fallen
feel	felt	felt
fight	fought	fought
find	found	found
fly	flew	flown
forget	forgot	forgotten
get	got	got
give	gave	given
go	went	gone
grow	grew	grown
have	had	had
hear	heard	heard
hit	hit	hit
hold	held	held
hurt	hurt	hurt
keep	kept	kept
know	knew	known
leave	left	left
let	let	let
lose	lost	lost
make	made	made
meet	met	met
pay	paid	paid
put	put	put
read	read	read
ring	rang	rung
ride	rode	ridden
run	ran	run
say	said	said
see	saw	seen
sell	sold	sold
send	sent	sent
shut	shut	shut
sing	sang	sung
sit	sat	sat
sleep	slept	slept
speak	spoke	spoken

Base form	Past simple	Past participle
spend	spent	spent
stand	stood	stood
steal	stole	stolen
swim	swam	swum
take	took	taken
teach	taught	taught
tell	told	told
think	thought	thought
understand	understood	understood
wake	woke	woken
wear	wore	worn
win	won	won
write	wrote	written

Phonetic symbols

Consonants	
/p/	pen
/b/	be
/t/	two
/d/	do
/k/	can
/g/	good
/f/	five
/v/	very
/m/	make
/n/	nice
/ŋ/	sing
/s/	see
/z/	trousers
/w/	we
/l/	listen
/r/	right
/j/	you
/h/	he
/θ/	thing
/ð/	this
/ʃ/	she
/tʃ/	cheese
/ʒ/	usually
/dʒ/	German

Vowels	
/æ/	man
/ɑː/	father
/e/	ten
/ɜː/	thirteen
/ə/	mother
/ɪ/	sit
/iː/	see
/ʊ/	book
/uː/	food
/ʌ/	up
/ɒ/	hot
/ɔː/	four

Diphthongs	
/eɪ/	great
/aɪ/	fine
/ɔɪ/	boy
/ɪə/	hear
/eə/	chair
/aʊ/	town
/əʊ/	go
/ʊə/	pure

Wordlist

(v) = verb   (n) = noun   (adj) = adjective   (adv) = adverb

Unit 1

Giving statistics and making generalisations

1 in 3 /wən ɪn 'θriː/
two thirds of /tuː 'θɜːdz əv/
a lot of /ə 'lɒt əv/
half of /'hɑːf əv/
it is (un)common for /ɪt ɪz 'kɒmən fər/
just over /ˌdʒʌst 'əʊvər/
just under /ˌdʒʌst 'ʌndər/
more and more /'mɔːr ənd 'mɔːr/
most /məʊst/
a quarter of /ə 'kwɔːtər əv/
ten percent (10%) of /ten pə'sent əv/
the majority of /ðə mə'dʒɒrəti əv/

Making new friends

bond with (v) /'bɒnd wɪð/
feel left out (v) /fiːl left 'aʊt/
fit in (v) /fɪt 'ɪn/
join in (v) /dʒɔɪn 'ɪn/
settle in (v) /ˌsetl 'ɪn/

Foreign culture

continent (n) /'kɒntɪnənt/
culture (n) /'kʌltʃər/
dialect (n) /'daɪəlekt/
emigrate (v) /'emɪɡreɪt/
foreign (adj) /'fɒrɪn/
immigrant (n) /'ɪmɪɡrənt/
immigrate (v) /'ɪmɪɡreɪt/
immigration (n) /ˌɪmɪ'ɡreɪʃən/
invade (v) /ɪn'veɪd/

Adjectives

contemporary /kən'tempərəri/
emotional /ɪ'məʊʃənəl/
rhythmical /'rɪðmɪkəl/
suburban /sə'bɜːbən/
traditional /trə'dɪʃənəl/
war-torn /'wɔːr ˌtɔːn/

Nouns

entertainment /ˌentə'teɪnmənt/
environment /ɪn'vaɪərənmənt/
percentage /pə'sentɪdʒ/
poem /'pəʊəm/
poet /'pəʊɪt/

politics /'pɒlətɪks/
population /ˌpɒpjə'leɪʃən/
report /rɪ'pɔːt/
representation /ˌreprɪzen'teɪʃən/
statistic (n) /stə'tɪstɪk/
teen /tiːn/
trend /trend/

Verbs

adapt /ə'dæpt/
earn /ɜːn/
find out /faɪnd 'aʊt/
increase /ɪn'kriːs/
prefer /prɪ'fɜːr/
tend to /'tend tuː/

Unit 2

Communication

body contact (n) /'bɒdi ˌkɒntækt/
body language (n) /'bɒdi ˌlæŋɡwɪdʒ/
communicate (v) /kə'mjuːnɪkeɪt/
cross your arms (v) /ˌkrɒs jər 'ɑːmz/
deaf (adj) /def/
eye contact (n) /'aɪ ˌkɒntækt/
gesture (v, n) /'dʒestʃər/
give a warm smile (v) /ɡɪv ə wɔːm 'smaɪl/
lean forward (v) /liːn 'fɔːwəd/
look (nervous) (v) /lʊk/
nod your head (v) /nɒd jə 'hed/
raise your eyebrows (v) /reɪz jɔːr 'aɪbraʊz/
sign (v) /saɪn/
sign language (n) /'saɪn ˌlæŋɡwɪdʒ/
sit back (v) /sɪt 'bæk/

say and tell

say a prayer /seɪ ə 'preɪər/
say goodbye /seɪ ɡʊd'baɪ/
say (something) again /seɪ ə'ɡen/
say (something) out loud /seɪ aʊt 'laʊd/
say sorry /seɪ 'sɒri/
say thank you /seɪ 'θæŋk juː/
tell a joke /tel ə 'dʒəʊk/
tell a lie /tel ə 'laɪ/

tell a secret /tel ə 'siːkrət/
tell a story /tel ə 'stɔːri/
tell (someone) off /tel 'ɒf/
tell the difference /tel ðə 'dɪfərənts/
tell the time /tel ðə 'taɪm/
tell the truth /tel ðə 'truːθ/

Phrasal verbs with up

break up /breɪk 'ʌp/
look (someone) up /lʊk 'ʌp/
meet up /miːt 'ʌp/
turn up /tɜːn 'ʌp/

Adjectives

unsure /ʌn'ʃɔːr/

Nouns

accent /'æksənt/
drive-thru /'draɪvθruː/
emergency service /ɪˌmɜːdʒəntsi 'sɜːvɪs/
employee /emplɔɪ'iː/
event /ɪ'vent/
kindergarten /'kɪndəˌɡaːtən/
knowledge /'nɒlɪdʒ/
learning disabilities /'lɜːnɪŋ dɪsəˌbɪlətiz/
opportunity /ˌɒpə'tjuːnəti/
relationship /rɪ'leɪʃənʃɪp/

Verbs

avoid /ə'vɔɪd/
borrow /'bɒrəʊ/
bump into /bʌmp 'ɪntə/
invite /ɪn'vaɪt/
lose touch with /luːz 'tʌtʃ wɪð/
plan /plæn/
raise /reɪz/
work out /wɜːk aʊt/

Everyday English

all right, mate? /ɔːl 'raɪt 'meɪt/
anyway /'eniweɪ/
got to be going /ɡɒt tuː biː 'ɡəʊɪŋ/
how's life? /haʊz 'laɪf/
long time, no see /'lɒŋ taɪm nəʊ 'siː/
nice seeing you /'naɪs 'siːɪŋ juː/
take care /'teɪk keər/

Unit 3

Friends and enemies

fall out with (someone) (v) /fɔːl 'aʊt wɪð/
get on (well) with (someone) (v) /ɡet 'ɒn wɪð/
let (someone) down (v) /let 'daʊn/
stand by (someone) (v) /stænd 'baɪ/
stick up for (someone) (v) /stɪk 'ʌp fə/
tell on (someone) (v) /'tel ɒn/

Adjectives

considerate /kən'sɪdərət/
faithful /'feɪθfəl/
fast-flowing /faːst 'fləʊɪŋ/

Adverbs

furiously /'fjʊəriəsli/

Nouns

apple pie /ˌæpl 'paɪ/
audience /'ɔːdiənts/
background /'bækɡraʊnd/
bridge /brɪdʒ/
crowd /kraʊd/
darkness /'daːknəs/
gentleness /'dʒentlnəs/
microphone /'maɪkrəfəʊn/
mile /maɪl/
programmer /'prəʊɡræmər/
suitcase /'suːtkeɪs/
supper /'sʌpər/
valley /'væli/

Verbs

argue /'aːɡjuː/
bark /baːk/
cheer /tʃɪər/
damage /'dæmɪdʒ/
discover /dɪ'skʌvər/
explain /ɪk'spleɪn/
hug /hʌɡ/
injure /'ɪndʒər/
introduce /ˌɪntrə'djuːs/
pat /pæt/
persuade /pə'sweɪd/
promise /'prɒmɪs/
surf the Internet /sɜːf ðə 'ɪntənet/
take a deep breath /teɪk ə diːp 'breθ/
wonder /'wʌndər/

Unit 4

Jobs and work

advertisement (n) /əd'vɜːtɪsmənt/
apply for a job (v) /ə,plaɪ fər ə 'dʒɒb/
application form (n) /,æplɪ'keɪʃən fɔːm/
badly-paid (adj) /,bædli 'peɪd/
banking (n) /'bæŋkɪŋ/
career (n) /kə'rɪər/
company (n) /'kʌmpəni/
contract (n) /'kɒntrækt/
CV (n) /,siː'viː/
employee (n) /emplɔɪ'iː/
employer (n) /ɪm'plɔɪər/
fill in a form (v) /fɪl ɪn ə 'fɔːm/
full-time (adj) /,fʊl'taɪm/
Information Technology (n) /,ɪnfə'meɪʃən tek'nɒlədʒi/
interview (v, n) /'ɪntəvjuː/
part-time (adj) /,pɑːt'taɪm/
qualification (n) /,kwɒlɪfɪ'keɪʃən/
resign (v) /rɪ'zaɪn/
salary (n) /'sæləri/
sales assistant (n) /'seɪlz ə,sɪstənt/
sign a contract (v) /saɪn ə 'kɒntrækt/
skills (n) /skɪlz/
trainee (n) /,treɪ'niː/
unemployed (adj) /,ʌnɪm'plɔɪd/
web designer (n) /'web dɪ,zaɪnər/
well-paid (adj) /wel 'peɪd/

Adjectives

ambitious /æm'bɪʃəs/
challenging /'tʃælɪndʒɪŋ/
current /'kʌrənt/
fascinating /'fæsɪneɪtɪŋ/
official /ə'fɪʃəl/
rewarding /rɪ'wɔːdɪŋ/

Nouns

advice /əd'vaɪs/
agent /'eɪdʒənt/
autograph /'ɔːtəgrɑːf/
degree /dɪ'griː/
delicatessen /,delɪkə'tesən/
gig /gɪg/
fame /feɪm/
industry /'ɪndəstri/
intention /ɪn'tentʃən/
record /'rekɔːd/
software /'sɒftweər/
soul /səʊl/
success /sək'ses/

Verbs

admire /əd'maɪər/
create /kri'eɪt/
enclose /ɪn'kləʊz/

Unit 5

Travel and movement

arrive at (v) /ə'raɪv ət/
arrive in (v) /ə'raɪv ɪn/
boarding card (n) /'bɔːdɪŋ kɑːd/
check-in desk (n) /'tʃek ɪn desk/
check in (v) /tʃek 'ɪn/
cruise (v, n) /kruːz/
customs (n) /'kʌstəmz/
depart (from) (v) /dɪ'pɑːt/
departure lounge (n) /dɪ'pɑːtʃər laʊndʒ/
flight (n) /flaɪt/
get on (a plane/train/bus/bike) (v) /get ɒn/
get in (the car / a taxi) (v) /get ɪn/
head for (v) /həd fə/
journey (n) /'dʒɜːni/
miss (the flight) (v) /mɪs/
passport (n) /'pɑːspɔːt/
platform (n) /'plætfɔːm/
take off (v) /teɪk 'ɒf/
terminal (n) /'tɜːmɪnəl/
timetable (n) /'taɪm,teɪbl/
travel (v) /'trævəl/
trip (n) /trɪp/
touch down (v) /tʌtʃ 'daʊn/
tour (n) /tʊər/

Adjectives

exhausted /ɪg'zɔːstɪd/
geomagnetic /,dʒiː:əʊmæg'netɪk/
minor /'maɪnər/
single-handed /,sɪŋgl'hændɪd/
smooth /smuːð/
solo /'səʊləʊ/
transatlantic /,trænzət'læntɪk/
worthwhile /,wɜːθ'hwaɪl/

Nouns

adventurer /əd'ventʃərər/
ambition /æm'bɪʃən/
astronaut /'æstrənɔːt/
atmosphere /'ætməsfɪər/
cosmonaut /'kɒzmənɔːt/
courage /'kʌrɪdʒ/
determination /dɪ,tɜːmɪ'neɪʃən/
equipment /ɪ'kwɪpmənt/
mast /mɑːst/
nation /'neɪʃən/
personality /,pɜːsən'æləti/
pity /'pɪti/

sailor /'seɪlər/
spaceship /'speɪsʃɪp/
sponsorship /'spɒntsəʃɪp/
sunburn /'sʌnbɜːn/
sunrise /'sʌnraɪz/
surface /'sɜːfɪs/
trimaran /'traɪməræn/
yacht /jɒt/

Verbs

compete /kəm'piːt/
invest /ɪn'vest/
recover /rɪ'kʌvər/
repair /rɪ'peər/

Unit 6

Artificial intelligence

artificial (adj) /,ɑːtɪ'fɪʃəl/
blind (adj) /blaɪnd/
brain (n) /breɪn/
computer chip /kəm'pjuːtə tʃɪp/
consciousness (n) /'kɒnʃəsnəs/
develop (v) /dɪ'veləp/
disease (n) /dɪ'ziːz/
download (v) /,daʊn'ləʊd/
drug (n) /drʌg/
electronic (adj) /,elek'trɒnɪk/
gene (n) /dʒiːn/
genetic (adj) /dʒə'netɪk/
homepage (n) /'həʊmpeɪdʒ/
immortality (n) /,ɪmɔː'tæləti/
intelligence (n) /ɪn'telɪdʒəns/
invention (n) /ɪn'ventʃən/
memory (n) /'meməri/
recognise (v) /'rekəgnaɪz/
research (n) /'rɪsɜːtʃ/
research (v) /rɪ'sɜːtʃ/
speech pattern (n) /'spiːtʃ ,pætən/
virtual hostess (n) /,vɜːtʃuəl həʊ'stes/

Time conjunctions

as soon as /æz suːn æz/
if /ɪf/
unless /ən'les/
until /ən'tɪl/
when /wen/

Verbs with prepositions

argue with (someone) /'ɑːgjuː wɪð/
get ready for (school) /get 'redi fɔːr/
revise for (exams) /rɪ'vaɪz fɔːr/
think about (something) /'θɪŋk ə,baʊt/

worry about (something) /'wʌri ə,baʊt/

Phrasal verbs with *into*

bump into /bʌmp 'ɪntə/
go into /gəʊ 'ɪntə/
look into /lʊk 'ɪntə/
turn into /tɜːn 'ɪntə/

Adjectives

entire /ɪn'taɪər/
human /'hjuːmən/
similar /'sɪmɪlə/
upset /ʌp'set/
visible /'vɪzəbl/

Nouns

author /'ɔːθər/
life style /'laɪf staɪl/
Parkinson's disease /'pɑːkɪnsənz dɪ'ziːz/
planet /'plænɪt/
vitamin (n) /'vɪtəmɪn/

Verbs

argue /'ɑːgjuː/
burn /bɜːn/
compose /kəm'pəʊz/
conclude /kən'kluːd/
crash /kræʃ/
investigate /ɪn'vestɪgeɪt/
rescue /'reskjuː/

Everyday English

believe it or not /bɪ'liːv ɪt ɔː nɒt/
between you and me /bɪ'twiːn juː ənd miː/
I know what you mean /aɪ 'nəʊ hwɒt juː 'miːn/
the fact is /ðə 'fækt ɪz/

Unit 7

make and *do*

do (a lot of) good /duː 'gʊd/
do your best /duː jə 'best/
make a difference /meɪk ə 'dɪfərəns/
make a mess /meɪk ə 'mes/
make an effort /meɪk æn 'efət/
make fun of (someone) /meɪk 'fʌn əv/
make money /meɪk 'mʌni/
make progress /meɪk 'prəʊgres/
make room /meɪk 'ruːm/
make sense /meɪk 'sens/

Adjectives

alternative /ɔːl'tɜːnətɪv/
endangered /ɪn'deɪndʒəd/
halfway /,hɑːf'weɪ/

nomadic /nəʊ'mædɪk/
peaceful /'piːsfəl/
self-sufficient
    /ˌselfsə'fɪʃənt/
tribal /'traɪbəl/

Nouns

authority /ɔː'θɒrəti/
campaign /kæm'peɪn/
developer /dɪ'veləpər/
development /dɪ'veləpmənt/
effect /ɪ'fekt/
fingerprint /'fɪŋgəprɪnt/
fund /fʌnd/
inspector /ɪn'spektər/
motorway /'məʊtəweɪ/
murder /'mɜːdər/
quality /'kwɒləti/
settlement /'setlmənt/
suicide /'suːɪsaɪd/
supporter /sə'pɔːtər/
threat /θret/
townspeople /'taʊnzˌpiːpl/
tribe /traɪb/

Verbs

achieve /ə'tʃiːv/
announce /ə'naʊnts/
appeal /ə'piːl/
criticise /'krɪtɪsaɪz/
identify /aɪ'dentɪfaɪ/
install /ɪn'stɔːl/
shave /ʃeɪv/

Unit 8

Television

audience (n) /'ɔːdiəns/
celebrity (n) /sə'lebrəti/
contestant (n) /kən'testənt/
episode (n) /'epɪsəʊd/
presenter (n) /prɪ'zentər/
producer (n) /prə'djuːsər/
quiz show (n) /kwɪz ʃəʊ/
reality TV (n) /ri'æləti
    tiː'viː/
series (n) /'sɪəriːz/
sitcom (n) /'sɪtkɒm/
soap opera (n) /'səʊpˌɒprə/
spectator (n) /spek'teɪtər/
TV regulator (n) /ˌtiːviː
    'regjəleɪtər/
TV studio (n) /ˌtiːviː
    'stjuːdiəʊ/
viewer (n) /'vjuːər/
viewing figures (n) /'vjuːɪŋ
    ˌfɪgərz/

Collocations with *on*

on holiday /ɒn 'hɒlədeɪ/
on offer /ɒn 'ɒfər/
on strike /ɒn 'straɪk/
on the phone /ɒn ðə 'fəʊn/
on time /ɒn 'taɪm/
on TV /ɒn tiː'viː/

Adjectives

awake /ə'weɪk/
boiling /'bɔɪlɪŋ/
enormous /ɪ'nɔːməs/
exhausted /ɪk'sɔːstɪd/
fantastic /fæn'tæstɪk/
fictional /'fɪkʃənl/
freezing /'friːzɪŋ/
paranoid /'pærənɔɪd/
psychological
    /ˌsaɪkəl'ɒdʒɪkəl/
reasonable /'riːzənəbl/
tiny /'taɪni/
unpleasant /ʌn'plezənt/

Nouns

cave /keɪv/
complaint /kəm'pleɪnt/
harm /hɑːm/
health /helθ/
humiliation /hjuːˌmɪli'eɪʃən/
item /'aɪtəm/
limit /'lɪmɪt/
popularity /ˌpɒpjə'lærəti/
privacy /'prɪvəsi/
psychologist /saɪ'kɒlədʒɪst/
risk /rɪsk/
tuition /tju'ɪʃən/
twilight zone /'twaɪlaɪt
    zəʊn/
uniform /'juːnɪfɔːm/

Verbs

degrade /dɪ'greɪd/
reflect /rɪ'flekt/
reveal /rɪ'viːl/
vote /vəʊt/

Unit 9

Noun suffixes

agreement /ə'griːmənt/
difference /'dɪfərəns/
enjoyment /ɪn'dʒɔɪmənt/
entertainment
    /ˌentə'teɪnmənt/
imagination
    /ɪˌmædʒɪ'neɪʃən/
kindness /'kaɪndnəs/
popularity /ˌpɒpjə'lærəti/
possibility /ˌpɒsə'bɪləti/
preference /'prefərəns/
preparation /ˌprepər'eɪʃən/
reaction /ri'ækʃən/
relaxation /ˌriːlæk'seɪʃən/
shyness /'ʃaɪnəs/

Graffiti

burner (n) /'bɜːnər/
crew (n) /kruː/
graffiti (n) /grə'fiːti/
hip-hop scene (n) /'hɪphɒp
    siːn/
masterpiece (n)
    /'mɑːstəpiːs/

mixture (n) /'mɪkstʃər/
piece (n) /piːs/
portrait (n) /'pɔːtrɪt/
scheme (n) /skiːm/
spray (v, n) /spreɪ/
style wars (n) /'staɪl wɔːz/
subway (n) /'sʌbweɪ/
tag (v, n) /tæg/
talent (n) /'tælənt/
territory (n) /'terɪtəri/
throw up (n) /'θrəʊ ʌp/
vandalism (n) /'vændəlɪzəm/
writer (n) /'raɪtər/

Belonging to a group

feel left out by (someone) (v)
    /fiːl left 'aʊt baɪ/
hang out with (someone) (v)
    /hæŋ 'aʊt wɪð/
hook up with (someone) (v)
    /hʊk 'ʌp wɪð/
look up to (someone) (v) /lʊk
    'ʌp tuː/
relate to (someone) (v)
    /rɪ'leɪt tuː/

Adjectives

cruel /'kruːəl/
depressed /dɪ'prest/
frustrated /frʌs'treɪtɪd/
inner-city /ˌɪnə'sɪti/
legal /'liːgəl/
stylish /'staɪlɪʃ/

Nouns

army /'ɑːmi/
council /'kaʊnsəl/
creation /kri'eɪʃən/
disadvantage
    /ˌdɪsəd'vɑːntɪdʒ/
gang /gæŋ/

Verbs

attack /ə'tæk/
compare /kəm'peər/
detest /dɪ'test/
display /dɪ'spleɪ/
prove /pruːv/
provide /prəʊ'vaɪd/
threaten /'θretən/
vandalise /'vændəlaɪz/

Unit 10

Crime

arson (n) /'ɑːsən/
break the law (v) /breɪk ðə
    lɔː/
burglary (n) /'bɜːgləri/
commit a crime (v) /kəˌmɪt ə
    'kraɪm/
convicted (adj) /kɒn'vɪktɪd/
community service (n)
    /kəˌmjuːnəti 'sɜːvɪs/
criminal (n) /'krɪmɪnəl/

get away with (something)
    /get ə'weɪ wɪð/
get caught (v) /get 'kɔːt/
get into trouble (v) /get
    ˌɪntə 'trʌbl/
joyriding (n) /'dʒɔɪraɪdɪŋ/
pay a fine (v) /peɪ ə 'faɪn/
pick-pocketing (n) /'pɪk
    ˌpɒkətɪŋ/
prison (n) /'prɪzən/
probation (n) /prəʊ'beɪʃən/
punishment (n)
    /'pʌnɪʃmənt/
shoplifting (n) /'ʃɒplɪftɪŋ/
vandalism (n) /'vændəlɪzəm/

Phrasal verbs with *down*

break down /breɪk 'daʊn/
get (someone) down /get
    'daʊn/
slow down /sləʊ 'daʊn/
turn (something) down /tɜːn
    'daʊn/

Adjectives

alarming /ə'lɑːmɪŋ/
honest /'ɒnɪst/
secondhand /ˌsekənd'hænd/

Nouns

boredom /'bɔːdəm/
community /kə'mjuːnəti/
option /'ɒpʃən/
responsibility
    /rɪˌspɒntsə'bɪləti/
rubbish /'rʌbɪʃ/
society /sə'saɪəti/
solution /sə'luːʃən/

Verbs

leave school /liːv 'skuːl/
lend /lend/
make up an excuse /meɪk ʌp
    ən ɪk'skjuːs/
owe /əʊ/

Everyday English

and besides /ænd bɪ'saɪdz/
that's a good point /'ðæts ə
    gʊd ˌpɔɪnt/
the way I see it /ðə weɪ 'aɪ
    siː ɪt/
you never know /jə 'nevə
    nəʊ/

Unit 11

Linkers of contrast

although /ɔːl'ðəʊ/
despite /dɪ'spaɪt/
even though /ˌiːvən 'ðəʊ/
however /haʊ'evər/
in spite of /ɪn 'spaɪt əv/

Problems

come back to it (v) /kʌm ˈbæk tuː ɪt/
come up (v) /kʌm ˈʌp/
come up with (v) /kʌm ʌp wɪð/
go away (v) /gəʊ əˈweɪ/
ignore (v) /ɪgˈnɔːr/
make up your mind (v) /meɪk ʌp jə ˈmaɪnd/
sleep on it (v) /ˈsliːp ɒn ɪt/
sort it out (v) /sɔːt ɪt ˈaʊt/
talk it over (v) /tɔːk ɪt ˈəʊvər/
think it over (v) /θɪŋk ɪt ˈəʊvər/

Adjectives

confident /ˈkɒnfɪdənt/
decisive /dɪˈsaɪsɪv/
deserted /dezˈɜːtɪd/
extinct /ɪkˈstɪŋkt/
hypnotic /hɪpˈnɒtɪk/
immediate /ɪˈmiːdiət/
incredible /ɪnˈkredɪbl/
luxurious /lʌgˈʒʊəriəs/
native /ˈneɪtɪv/
remote /rɪˈməʊt/
stressful /ˈstresfʊl/
tropical /ˈtrɒpɪkəl/
unfortunate /ʌnˈfɔːtʃənət/
unspoiled /ʌnˈspɔɪlt/
wooden /ˈwʊdən/

Nouns

ambulance /ˈæmbjələns/
bulldozer /ˈbʊlˌdəʊzər/
coconut palm /ˈkəʊkənʌt pɑːm/
conspiracy theory /kənˈspɪrəsi ˌθɪəri/
coral reef /ˈkɒrəl riːf/
crater /ˈkreɪtər/
hypnotist /ˈhɪpnətɪst/
inhabitant /ɪnˈhæbɪtənt/
landscape /ˈlændskeɪp/
monsoon /mɒnˈsuːn/
moon buggy /ˈmuːn ˌbʌgi/
resort /rɪˈzɔːt/
sand /sænd/
shadow /ˈʃædəʊ/
source /sɔːs/
telescope /ˈtelɪskəʊp/

Verbs

discuss /dɪˈskʌs/
forbid /fəˈbɪd/
hypnotise /ˈhɪpnətaɪz/
live life to the full /laɪv ˌlaɪf tuː ðə ˈfʊl/
pollute /pəˈluːt/
shock /ʃɒk/
undo /ʌnˈduː/
whisper /ˈwɪspər/

Unit 12

Phrasal verbs

call off /kɔːl ˈɒf/
come across /kʌm əˈkrɒs/
go out /gəʊ ˈaʊt/
pay off /peɪ ˈɒf/
pass away /pɑːs əˈweɪ/
start out /stɑːt ˈaʊt/
talk (someone) into (something) /tɔːk ˈɪntə/
tie in with /taɪ ˈɪn wɪð/

Expressions with *be* + preposition

be against (something) /biː əˈgentst/
be off (something) /biː ˈɒf/
be onto (something/someone) /biː ˈɒntə/

Adjectives

buried /ˈberid/
decorative /ˈdekərətɪv/
eternal /ɪˈtɜːnəl/
holy /ˈhəʊli/
meaningless /ˈmiːnɪŋləs/
volcanic /vɒlˈkænɪk/

Nouns

apparition /æpərˈɪʃən/
archaeologist /ˌɑːkiˈɒlədʒɪst/
blessing /ˈblesɪŋ/
cruelty /ˈkruːəlti/
curse /kɜːs/
destiny /ˈdestɪni/
discovery /dɪˈskʌvəri/
doubt /daʊt/
favour /ˈfeɪvər/
ghost /gəʊst/
inscription /ɪnˈskrɪpʃən/
mummy /ˈmʌmi/
ornament /ˈɔːnəmənt/
passageway /ˈpæsɪdʒweɪ/
profession /prəˈfeʃən/
pyramid /ˈpɪrəmɪd/
runway /ˈrʌnweɪ/
statue /ˈstætʃuː/

Verbs

cancel /ˈkænsəl/
disturb /dɪˈstɜːb/
misunderstand /ˌmɪsʌndəˈstænd/
persuade /pəˈsweɪd/
reach /riːtʃ/

Unit 13

Appearance

afro (n) /ˈæfrəʊ/
beard (n) /bɪəd/
bushy (adj) /ˈbʊʃi/
broad shouldered (adj) /brɔːd ˈʃəʊldəd/
centre parting (n) /ˌsentər ˈpɑːtɪŋ/
clean shaven (adj) /kliːn ˈʃeɪvən/
cropped (adj) /krɒpt/
double chin (n) /ˌdʌbl ˈtʃɪn/
eyebrows (n) /ˈaɪbraʊz/
eyelashes (n) /ˈaɪlæʃɪz/
freckles (n) /ˈfreklz/
fringe (n) /frɪndʒ/
highlights (n) /ˈhaɪlaɪts/
medium height (adj) /ˌmiːdiəm ˈhaɪt/
mole (n) /məʊl/
moustache (n) /məˈstɑːʃ/
plump (adj) /plʌmp/
ponytail (n) /ˈpəʊniteɪl/
rosy cheeks (n) /ˌrəʊzi ˈtʃiːks/
scar (n) /skɑːr/
slim (n) /slɪm/
spiky (adj) /ˈspaɪki/
spots (n) /spɒts/
tattoo (n) /tætˈuː/
wavy (adj) /ˈweɪvi/
well-built (adj) /ˌwelˈbɪlt/
wrinkles (n) /ˈrɪŋklz/

Personality

ambitious (adj) /æmˈbɪʃəs/
bad-tempered (adj) /ˌbædˈtempəd/
bossy (adj) /ˈbɒsi/
considerate (adj) /kənˈsɪdərət/
determined (adj) /dɪˈtɜːmɪnd/
imaginative (adj) /ɪˈmædʒɪnətɪv/
independent (adj) /ˌɪndɪˈpendənt/
insensitive (adj) /ɪnˈsensətɪv/
sensible (adj) /ˈsensɪbl/
sensitive (adj) /ˈsensɪtɪv/

Reporting verbs

agree /əˈgriː/
apologise for /əˈpɒlədʒaɪz fər/
ask /ɑːsk/
beg /beg/
explain /ɪkˈspleɪn/
invite /ɪnˈvaɪt/
offer /ˈɒfər/
order /ˈɔːdər/
persuade /pəˈsweɪd/
refuse /ˈrefjuːs/
say /seɪ/
suggest /səˈdʒest/
tell /tel/

Relationships

break up (v) /breɪk ˈʌp/
fall in love with (someone) (v) /fɔːl ɪn ˈlʌv wɪð/
get back together (v) /get bæk təˈgeðər/
get divorced (v) /get dɪˈvɔːst/
get engaged (v) /get ɪnˈgeɪdʒd/
get married (v) /get ˈmærid/
go out (together) (v) /gəʊ ˈaʊt/

Adjectives

sacred /ˈseɪkrɪd/
wealthy /ˈwelθi/

Nouns

best man /best ˈmæn/
bride /braɪd/
ceremony /ˈserɪməni/
desire /dɪˈzaɪər/
groom /gruːm/
mosque /mɒsk/
powder /ˈpaʊdər/
priest /priːst/
purity /ˈpjʊərəti/
Qur'an /kɒrˈɑːn/
sweetness /ˈswiːtnəs/
token /ˈtəʊkən/
witness /ˈwɪtnəs/

Verbs

bless /bles/
decorate /ˈdekəreɪt/
exchange /ɪksˈtʃeɪndʒ/
love /lʌv/
pray /preɪ/
symbolise /ˈsɪmbəlaɪz/

Unit 14

Anger

anger (n) /ˈæŋgər/
angry (adj) /ˈæŋgri/
bite (someone's) head off (v) /baɪt ˈhed ɒf/
calm (adj) /kɑːm/
cross (adj) /krɒs/
furious (adj) /ˈfjʊəriəs/
have a tantrum (v) /hæv ə ˈtæntrəm/
hot-headed (adj) /hɒt ˈhedɪd/
keep your cool (v) /kiːp jə ˌkuːl/
lose your temper (v) /luːz jə ˈtempər/

Adjectives

amused /əˈmjuːzd/
athletic /æθˈletɪk/
horrified /ˈhɒrɪfaɪd/
plain-looking /ˈpleɪnlʊkɪŋ/

Nouns

compassion /kəmˈpæʃən/
discussion /dɪˈskʌʃən/
idiot /ˈɪdiət/
jogger /ˈdʒɒgər/
mugger /ˈmʌgər/

Verbs

agree on /əˈgriː ɒn/
frighten /ˈfraɪtən/
launch /lɔːntʃ/
queue up /kjuː ˈʌp/
regret /rɪˈgret/
score /skɔːr/

Everyday English

in that case /ɪn ˈðæt keɪs/
the thing is /ðə ˈθɪŋ ɪz/
there's something I want to
    say /ðeərz ˌsʌmθɪŋ aɪ
    wɒnt tuː ˈseɪ/
what I mean is /wɒt aɪ
    ˈmiːn ɪz/

Unit 15

Adjectives with prefixes

illegal /ɪˈliːgəl/
illogical /ɪˈlɒdʒɪkəl/
impatient /ɪmˈpeɪʃənt/
impolite /ˌɪmpəˈlaɪt/

impossible /ɪmˈpɒsəbl/
inexpensive /ˌɪnɪkˈspensɪv/
informal /ɪnˈfɔːməl/
irregular /ɪˈregjələr/
irresponsible /ˌɪrɪˈspɒnsəbl/
unafraid /ˌʌnəˈfreɪd/
uncomfortable
    /ʌnˈkʌmpftəbl/
unhelpful /ʌnˈhelpfʊl/

Phrasal verbs with *sit*

sit back /sɪt ˈbæk/
sit for /ˈsɪt fə/
sit out /sɪt ˈaʊt/
sit through /sɪt θruː/

Adjectives

brave /breɪv/
circular /ˈsɜːkjələr/
creepy /ˈkriːpi/
cute /kjuːt/
guilty /ˈgɪlti/
mythical /ˈmɪθɪkəl/
ruined /ˈruːɪnd/
unrealistic /ˌʌnrɪəˈlɪstɪk/

Nouns

angle /ˈæŋgl/
audition /ɔːˈdɪʃən/
companion /kəmˈpænjən/
dozen /ˈdʌzən/
dwarf /dwɔːf/
elf /elf/

epic /ˈepɪk/
ghost /gəʊst/
legend /ˈledʒənd/
madness /ˈmædnəs/
performance /pəˈfɔːməns/
special effect /ˌspeʃəl
    ɪˈfekt/
suspense /səˈspens/
technique /tekˈniːk/
wardrobe /ˈwɔːdrəʊb/

Verbs

advertise /ˈædvətaɪz/
audition /ɔːˈdɪʃən/
deposit /dɪˈpɒzɪt/
release /rɪˈliːs/
scream /skriːm/
terrorise /ˈterəraɪz/

Unit 16

feel

feel confident /fiːl
    ˈkɒnfɪdənt/
feel fine /fiːl ˈfaɪn/
feel lonely /fiːl ˈləʊnli/
feel sorry for /fiːl ˈsɒri fər/
feel strange /fiːl ˈstreɪndʒ/
feel stupid /fiːl ˈstjuːpɪd/
feel the need /fiːl ðə ˈniːd/
feel up to (something) /fiːl
    ˈʌp tə/

Expressions with prepositions

in and out /ˈɪn ənd ˈaʊt/
on and on /gəʊ ɒn ənd ɒn/
on the up and up /ɒn ðə ˈʌp
    ənd ˈʌp/
through and through /ˈθruː
    ənd θruː/
up and about /ˈʌp ənd
    əˈbaʊt/
up and down /ˈʌp ənd
    daʊn/

Nouns

flow /fləʊ/
freedom /ˈfriːdəm/
humour /ˈhjuːmər/
siesta /siˈestə/

Verbs

achieve /əˈtʃiːv/
concentrate /ˈkɒnsəntreɪt/
give up /gɪv ˈʌp/
imply /ɪmˈplaɪ/
waste time /weɪst ˈtaɪm/

Unit 10, page 68, Exercise 2

Less than 8 points
You aren't really very honest. Do your friends lend you things? Probably not. Maybe you should ask yourself why.

13–8 points
You're often honest. You are the type of person who doesn't want to hurt their friends, so maybe you sometimes lie to be kind.

More than 13 points
Well done – you're perfect! But be careful you don't hurt your friends by being too honest!